NELSON

*An
Illustrated
History*

NELSON

An Illustrated History

ROGER MORRISS, BRIAN LAVERY AND STEPHEN DEUCHAR
Edited by PIETER VAN DER MERWE

Laurence King in association with the National Maritime Museum

Published 1995 by Laurence King Publishing
Copyright © 1995 The National Maritime Museum, Greenwich

A catalogue record for this book is available from the British Library.

ISBN 1 85669 061 X

Designed by *The Bridgewater Book Company*
Printed in Singapore by Toppan

FRONT COVER: Captain Nelson, by Rigaud (see page 62)
FRONTISPIECE: *The Immortality of Nelson*, by West (see page 155)

For our current catalogue, please write to:

LAURENCE KING PUBLISHING
71 Great Russell Street
London WC1B 3BN

For a catalogue of publications from
the National Maritime Museum, please write to:

NATIONAL MARITIME MUSEUM
Greenwich
London SE10 9NF

The National Maritime Museum gratefully acknowledges
the support of the following in the redevelopment of its NELSON Gallery, 1995:

SUN ALLIANCE
LLOYD'S OF LONDON

Trafalgar Gallery, Harrogate
Warwick Leadlay, Greenwich

February 1995

CONTENTS

Horatio, Viscount Nelson,
Vice-Admiral of the White,
(1758-1805) by Lemuel Francis
Abbott (1760-1803). The best of
a number of versions painted in
1797 when he was a rear-admiral.

FOREWORD

*N*EW BOOKS on Nelson are published every year, often prefaced with an author's apology: he (or she) hesitates to add another to the ever-growing pile *but...*and reasons are given for telling the famous story again.

Whatever the merits of this addition, no such apology is offered for it. The National Maritime Museum holds the world's greatest collections on Nelson and the Royal Navy of his time – in paintings, personal relics, manuscripts and all other types of material. And yet, while much of this is often reproduced, the Museum has so far published nothing more substantial than a 28-page booklet on Nelson in its sixty-year history.

There are two reasons for doing so now. First, this book accompanies the Museum's latest Nelson gallery, the third major redisplay on the subject since World War II. Not everything in the gallery is in these pages, or vice versa, but they reflect a broadly similar approach to the subject. More items from the Museum's Nelsonic holdings are also illustrated here than have ever appeared in one book before, together with relevant images from other sources. Second, both the gallery and the book mark the first year of the 'Nelson Decade' in which the Museum, with other interested parties, will be commemorating the great Nelson bicentenaries, culminating in that of the Battle of Trafalgar in 2005.

An illustrated work of this size cannot also be a full biography of Nelson or a detailed account of his naval achievements. The book gives an authoritative outline of both, however, and offers interpretations of those aspects which underlie Nelson's continuing appeal and place in Britain's national consciousness. The authors are members of the Museum staff with specific expertise and interest in matters related to Nelson and his times: Roger Morriss has written extensively on naval administration and biography in the period; Brian Lavery is author of several well-known books on its shipbuilding and shipboard organization; Stephen Deuchar is an art historian currently undertaking broader work on the place of Nelsonic imagery in British culture. Their contributions have been drawn together by Pieter van der Merwe, the Museum's General Editor. Many other members of the Museum are also due thanks for their contributions behind the scenes, notably Tina Chambers and Peter Robinson of the NMM Photographic Studio, and Christopher Gray in administering the complex photographic procurement, detailed and acknowledged on page 172. We are also very grateful to our publishers, Calmann and King, and their Senior Editor, Joanne Lightfoot, for their faith in the project and for bringing it to practical fruition.

RICHARD ORMOND
Director, National Maritime Museum, Greenwich

A TIME FOR HEROES

'THERE are a handful of characters whose interest seems to grow rather than diminish with the passage of time. Among men of war, Napoleon, Nelson and Wellington are ... those of whom it seems impossible to know too much...' ★

Nelson has been considered in many ways – as a great leader and hero, a martyr, a lover, an unfaithful husband, a personality, and as a medical and psychological case. At root, his historical importance lies in his record for delivering decisive naval victories at critical points during the longest major war Britain has fought in the modern era. At the same time, it is the tension between his professional achievements and his often extravagant public and private behaviour which makes him, in death as in life, such a fascinating figure.

The fact that Nelson's name is familiar worldwide, even among those who know nothing else of him, is a measure of his 'star' status. But it would be wrong to assume from this that he was either the world's greatest seaman or strategic thinker, or indeed an unmatched fighter. Robert Blake and Michiel de Ruyter, for example, were seventeenth-century fighting commanders one could name in the same breath, let alone some of Nelson's contemporaries. Drake and Cook had intrepidity and skills as navigators which Nelson was not required to show and he never reached the policy-making levels of an Anson, or more recently a Fisher or a Beatty; his own superior, the Earl of St Vincent, thought him unfitted to do so.

Such comparisons are crude but serve as warning to those admirers of Nelson who see him in isolation, as a phenomenon detachable from his own time because he appears so sympathetic in ours. He was one of a talented generation of Royal Naval officers and if his personal magnetism was unusual his experience and professional aspirations were not. His most unconventional attribute, and that perhaps one of degree rather than uniqueness, was a conviction of his destiny to be a hero and an unshakeable trust in God's mercy over his endeavours.

Nelson's personal and even child-like sense of heroic mission contributed to some of his failings, as well as underlying his virtues. His ambition, charm and skills as a leader were matched by a capacity for self-righteousness and exhibitionism which did him professional harm. His own admirable dash and defiance of physical danger sometimes led to unnecessary casualties. While notably kind, and humane by the standards of his time, he was also capable of making savagely questionable decisions, of which some of his actions at Naples in 1799 and his treatment of his wife are examples. As a daring and innovative squadron commander he was exceptional. In more complex circumstances, where military dispositions met political ones, his feelings

★ Oliver Warner, *Nelson's Last Diary* (1971), 20.

Napoleon portrayed as romantic hero at the
Battle of Arcola, Lombardy, in November
1796, where his defeat of the Austrians left
northern Italy in French hands. After the
portrait by Baron Gros, in the Louvre.

and convictions could undermine his judgement. It was fortunate that his successes outweighed his failures because he found criticism and censure, of which he attracted a considerable amount, almost impossible to accept.

One thing is certain: Nelson lived through events which produced heroes in a mould still appreciated today by a broad public. An aspect of the age of revolutions in which he lived was the rise of Romanticism in all aspects of European cultural outlook. As manifested in the arts and literature, the great social upheavals of the time were reflected in the image of individuals cast against apparently ungovernable forces, natural or man-made. In such a scenario, even the 'common man' was a candidate for spiritual nobility and heroic stature in his own landscape, and important public figures even more so.

Of figures perceived in this way, both then and later, the greatest in terms of overall impact was Napoleon Bonaparte. Born in 1769 and eleven years younger than Nelson, his rise from a similarly remote corner of provincial society was even more rapid: first as a military hero of Republican France and then, in 1804, completing its transformation to his own vision of a latter-day Roman empire with himself as Emperor. If Nelson was a hero, Napoleon was one on a grander plan, and correspondingly feared and hated by those pitted against him. His empire survived only ten years but, ironically, its consequences for European as well as French history, especially in constitutional and legal terms, have had wider effects than the individual legacy of any commander who contributed to his defeat.

The other figure with whom, for perspective, Nelson should be remembered is the Duke of Wellington, born earlier in the same year as Napoleon and thus also eleven years Nelson's junior. The acclaim which greeted his victories

Arthur Wellesley, Duke of Wellington, (1769-1852): painted in Spain at the end of the Peninsular Campaign, about 1813, by Thomas Heaphy.

over the French in Spain, from 1808 to late 1813, and finally against Napoleon himself at Waterloo in 1815, was equal in sum to any granted Nelson. In many respects his achievement was also more sustained, on a more complex scale, and attained with larger but inherently less disciplined forces. When Wellington famously said his own men frightened him, he was not commenting on their fighting ability but on the capacity of his troops (and some senior officers) to run out of control in ways the fleet never had to face. The Navy had disciplinary difficulties in the 1790s but was essentially a homogeneous and well-ordered service, a foundation on which Nelson's victories were built. Wellington's achievement was not only his success in battle; it was to instil the overall discipline he needed for victory into the diverse, regimental and international army of which he took command and to establish and maintain regularity in long and ever-shifting lines of supply.

The men were alike in two key respects. As commanders they both had an almost infallible 'eye for ground': the ability to assess a tactical situation rapidly and deploy forces with maximum and often original effect. As leaders, though in different ways, they both inspired extraordinary confidence in those they commanded, not least by always being visibly in the forefront of action. Otherwise their differences were great. Nelson was emotional, charismatic, personally brave and expressly burning to 'be a hero'. Wellington was a master planner on the grand scale and in detail, and coolly imperturbable in the face of superior odds, though he was also a more engaging and

sociable personality than often painted. He too saw his life as a service to crown and country but without the religious associations of Nelson and, though pressed on the matter, he consistently rejected any personal sense of being heroic.

Admiral and general only met once, just before Nelson's death. Wellington's report of the brief encounter records his astonishment at Nelson's superficial absurdities and his equal admiration of the charm, intelligence and judgement which they concealed. He was not alone in such observation and it is this mercurial quality, and its consequences in both Nelson's public and private life, which is the key to his enduring appeal, even to those whose naval interests are slight.

Successful military leaders are often placed on pedestals, metaphorically as well as in stone or bronze. But broad public interest in them eventually fades unless they are distinguished for other reasons than martial prowess. Among British ranks, Nelson sustains that interest to a unique degree, equally as a hero and as a fallible human being. This book aims to outline how this balance of reputation was established and has continued, illustrating the story largely from the collections of the National Maritime Museum.

C H A P T E R 1

THE AGE OF REVOLUTIONS

O F A L L the events taking place in Europe during Nelson's lifetime, it was the struggle between alternative forms of government – revolutionary republicanism and its consequences, versus parliamentary monarchy – which was the most important to his reputation, both as a naval leader and as a national hero. When he died at the Battle of Trafalgar on 21 October 1805, much was seen to be at stake: firstly, the survival of Britain's fleet, its main line of defence against French invasion and Napoleonic tyranny; secondly, the threat to Britain's political stability, already subject to the strains of reformist movements and the social pressures created by agricultural and industrial revolution; thirdly, the security of Britain's colonial empire, upon which the country's wealth and power were thought to depend. On all these fronts Nelson's overall success gained its greatest significance in the contribution he made to protecting British liberty, as then understood, and the continuing evolutionary, rather than revolutionary, social and political development which has been one of modern Britain's most important characteristics.

'Extirpation of the Plagues of Egypt:- Destruction of Revolutionary Crocodiles.' *A political interpretation* *of the Battle of the Nile, 1798, with Nelson as queller of French republicanism, by James Gillray (1757-1815).*

THE REVOLUTION IN POLITICAL IDEAS

The long conflict between Britain and France from 1793 to 1815, which is often loosely called the 'Napoleonic Wars'[1], can be traced back to the Reformation and the break of Protestantism from the church of Rome. By the seventeenth century, the absolute power of a monarch, sanctioned and supported by divine authority, was also being questioned. In England this led to the Civil War and the execution of Charles I. Although the monarchy was later restored, the right of subjects to remove their ruler was vindicated in the work of John Locke following the 'Glorious Revolution' of 1688, when James II became the second British monarch to be deposed within forty years. The theme was taken up in Thomas Paine's *Common Sense* of 1776, at the start of the American War of Independence, and in his *Rights*

'Consequences of a Successful French Invasion.' *Gillray's print of 1810 shows Napoleon's cohorts setting up a guillotine and tearing down the Spanish Armada tapestries in the old House of Lords.*

George III (1738-1820) came to the throne in 1760. He is shown here in the uniform of a general at Windsor. By Sir William Beechey (1753-1839).

of Man of 1791, following the revolution in France.

The rational, secular approach to ideas of government which such work represented also found expression in the theory of 'utilitarianism', outlined in Britain by Jeremy Bentham in 1780, during the American War. Its founding principle was that the value of an institution – government included – could be measured by the benefit derived from it by the largest number of people: 'the greatest happiness of the greatest number'. Such ideas were to gain increasing currency during Nelson's lifetime and, even if the larger political implications were resisted in Britain, many areas of public life, including management of the Navy, saw their examination and tentative application.

Abroad, events took a more violent course. In 1783, the right of subjects to choose their rulers was established when Britain recognized the independence of its rebellious American colonies. Ironically, the United States was substantially assisted in its struggle for independence by France, Spain and Holland, all of which were to suffer the consequences of their own citizens adopting the same principle over the next two decades.

In France, in the first half of the eighteenth century, ideas of independence from an oppressive monarchy were expressed in the work of writers and political philosophers such as Voltaire, Montesquieu and Rousseau. These pent-up ideas were released in 1789 when King Louis XVI, facing national bankruptcy, summoned the French parliament, the States-General, which had not met since 1614. Initially driven by the need for greater efficiency and social justice, the resulting French Revolution was soon taken over by more extreme groups. Thousands of Frenchmen fled abroad to escape imprisonment or the guillotine, including many officers in the French navy. Carrying forward their crusade against monarchy and aristocracy through war with Austria, Prussia and Sardinia, France's

William Pitt the Younger (1759-1806) became Tory Prime Minister in 1783, aged 24, and apart from a period from 1801 to 1804 remained so to his death. Nelson called him 'the greatest Minister this country ever had and the honestest man'. Marble, after Joseph Nollekens.

Charles James Fox (1749-1806), rakish leader of the radical Whig opposition. Tory propaganda often portrayed him as in league with French revolutionaries. Marble, by Frederico Nicoli (active 1817-20).

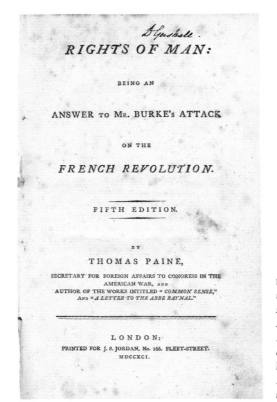

RIGHTS OF MAN:

BEING AN

ANSWER TO MR. BURKE's ATTACK

ON THE

FRENCH REVOLUTION.

FIFTH EDITION.

BY

THOMAS PAINE,

SECRETARY FOR FOREIGN AFFAIRS TO CONGRESS IN THE AMERICAN WAR, AND AUTHOR OF THE WORKS INTITLED "COMMON SENSE," AND "A LETTER TO THE ABBE RAYNAL."

LONDON:
PRINTED FOR J. S. JORDAN, No. 166, FLEET-STREET.
MDCCXCI.

LEFT Tom Paine was a notorious free-thinker and supporter of both the American and French Revolutions. The interest aroused by his Rights of Man (1791) led to eight English editions being printed in that year.

Guillotine blade and block, weighing 63.5lbs (28kg). Used to execute royalists on the French island of Guadeloupe, the guillotine from which this comes was captured by the Navy in 1794.

revolutionary armies began to overrun neighbouring countries. The execution of Louis XVI and the conquest of the southern Netherlands brought Britain into the war with France early in 1793.

REACTION TO REVOLUTION

In Britain the fear that revolution might cross the Channel set up a strong reaction against insurrectionary movements. In Parliament Edmund Burke led the assault against ideas that might weaken the balance of the existing constitution. According to this, the Crown still held considerable power to appoint ministers, either from the non-elected House of Lords or from the partially democratic House of Commons. The latter was already a target for reformers, who pointed out the geographically unequal distribution of seats and the unrepresentative electorate of many constituencies, owing to population growth. This was defended on the grounds that it provided 'virtual representation'.

A fear that small-scale changes might start a landslide into revolution led to the repression of reform efforts and drove much discontent underground. Working men who continued to agitate

'The Delegates in Counsel.' *The Nore mutineers portrayed as dupes of the French and the Opposition, headed by Fox, who lurk under the table.*

Richard, Earl Howe, Admiral of the Fleet (1726-99). Howe defeated the French in the first major sea battle of the war, in 1794, and peacefully negotiated an end to the Spithead mutiny through the respect in which seamen held him. By John Singleton Copley (1737-1815).

for reform, some taking the example of France as their model, were condemned as 'jacobins', the name of members of an extreme French Revolutionary political club. Their cause was helped by discontent arising from inflation, aggravated by sustained food shortages after 1795. The notorious Two Acts of December 1795 suppressed public meetings and condemned as treasonable any criticism of the king, the constitution and government in general. The Combination Laws of 1799-1800 later repressed trade union activity. In 1796 and 1797, open rebellion in Ireland attracted direct military support from France. In 1797 Britain's prime means of defence was threatened when a much feared mutiny took place in the fleet, first at Spithead and then at the Nore in the Thames Estuary (see page 46).

Nelson heard about much of this through his correspondence and copies of newspapers. At the time of the Spithead and Nore mutinies he was in England recovering from the loss of his right arm. He fully appreciated their danger to the fleet and the country and welcomed their forceful suppression. He was on shore over the winter of 1800-01, when food riots brought discontent to a head in the dockyard towns and

Richard Parker led the seamen's delegates in the Nore mutiny 'which created dreadful alarm through the whole Nation' according to this print, showing him as a French jacobin. He was hanged at the yardarm of the Sandwich, 30 June 1797.

RICHARD PARKER.

PRESIDENT of the DELEGATES in the late MUTINY in his MAJESTY'S FLEET at the NORE For which he suffer'd DEATH on board the SANDWICH the 30th of June 1797
York *Published as the act directs July 8th 1797 by J.Harrison & Co.*

ABOVE *The French warship* Droits de l'Homme *was returning troops to France from General Hoche's abortive invasion of Ireland in 1796, when the British frigates* Indefatigable *and* Amazon *drove her to destruction on the Brittany coast, 13 January 1797. Over 1,000 men died and the* Amazon *was also wrecked. From an engraving by Robert Dodd.*

necessitated that the military forces stationed in southern England be placed on alert, as much against internal rising as against invasion. Discontent never took wide hold; nor was it sufficiently well-organized to be a major threat to the British government. The forces against it were deceptively strong. Moreover, most radicals aimed to improve rather than destroy the existing system of democracy. There were deeply ingrained traditions of deference and paternalism, with a relatively comfortable and stable landed and farming community. The lower orders had opportunities to enlarge their earnings, if only on a small scale. There were also outlets for spiritual solace in growing non-conformist religious sects, as well as traditional means for those without formal influence in political life to vent their grievances and frustrations.

ADMINISTRATIVE AND SOCIAL REFORM

Political revolution in Britain was averted but this did not mean that change was not taking place. Indeed, it was growing expectations in society that encouraged political reformers. Public opinion was fuelled, from the 1760s, by the rise and widening circulation of newspapers. Transport imp-

rovements led to the development of a national network of local newspapers, influenced by the contents of the London press. The failure to hold the American colonies focused public attention on the apparent corruption that beset the administrative machinery of government. A traditional system of fee-taking, compensating for salary levels set in the seventeenth century, was equated with bribery and influence, apparently resulting in a debilitating waste of public funds. By 1800 a political movement aimed at 'economical reform' was already having some success in reducing the number of sinecures and unofficial payments, without which the business of many government departments would previously have been impossible.

Expectations were rising, too, in the field of social reform. Brutality pervaded almost all aspects of eighteenth-century society. Slavery and the slave trade were still condoned by large sections of the population. Many people, both

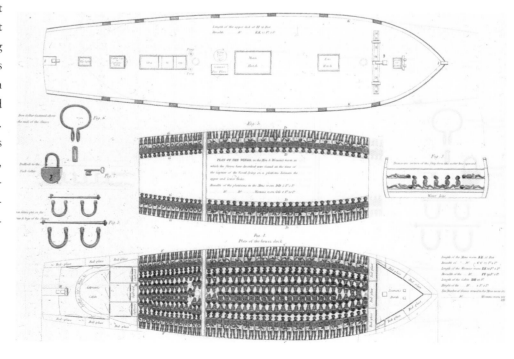

Lower deck of the Vigilante, *a French slaving brig, seized by the Navy in West Africa in 1822 with 345 slaves on board, chained in as shown.*

employers and workers, benefitted from making the trade goods with which slaves were bought in Africa. Britain also gained from the coffee, cotton and sugar produced by the slave economies of the West Indies and America. None the less, evangelical philanthropists, led in parliament by William Wilberforce, were gradually raising public feeling against the trade. Slave-owning in Britain had been declared legally inadmissible in 1772; further agitation and several parliamentary inquiries during the 1790s resulted in its abolition in British ships two years after Trafalgar.

The vulnerable within British society were also the subject of some consideration. Poverty, arising from increasing population, was endemic both in the countryside and in the rapidly growing towns. Nelson himself wrote sympathetically of the plight of agricultural labourers around Burnham Thorpe in 1792. In the agricultural south of England, where incentives to optimize crop growing and reduce labour costs were at their greatest, the end of the century saw the spread of 'poor relief' to those living outside the parish workhouses. However, such generosity as it allowed to poor people living in their own homes would eventually become intolerable to mean-minded rate-payers. Partly as a result of changes in agriculture, the rural poor began to move from the land into the towns. This did have one benefit: it fed the growth of industry, the Navy, and above all the army during wartime, at precisely the time when large-scale recruitment was necessary.

ECONOMIC CHANGE

These demographic changes sprang from far greater revolutions in the British economy than people could then conceive. The growth in population was itself an indication of the agricultural and industrial changes that were taking place.

During the eighteenth century the population of Britain roughly doubled, increasing from 5.5 to 10.5 million. London grew in proportion from about half a million to one million people.

Such numbers could not have been supported without greater efficiency in agriculture. The enclosure of common lands and establishment of consolidated holdings, consciously developed breeding patterns in animals and improved equipment such as cast-iron plough shares and threshing machinery — all these factors contributed to greater productivity. Inevitably some of the changes caused human distress. Yet, without them, population growth might only have been checked by the famine, disease and conflict still common in under-developed countries. Large-scale food production was also essential for supplying the Navy. In 1794 high food prices in Devon were explained by the presence of the fleet off Plymouth; local markets had to feed an additional 20,000 men, a number nearly equal to the area's population. After Devon had been drained of oxen, sheep, corn and potatoes, naval supplies were drawn from the counties of Somerset, Dorset, Gloucester and Worcester.

The growth and movement of the population, and changes in its employment, also reflected increasing industrial power. Much of the growth in industry took place in northern regions resourced by coal and iron, where established home-based skills could also supply large quantities of hand-woven woollen cloth. The steam engine was yet to make its full impact on textile manufacture but it was already used in mining and several other industries. The first steam engine used by the Navy appeared in Portsmouth dockyard in 1796 and, by the time of Trafalgar, steam dredgers were in use off Deptford dockyard on the Thames, and in Portsmouth harbour.

'Dark satanic mills': the awesome excitement of early industrialization is captured in this 1801 night view of the iron foundries of Coalbrookdale, by Philippe-Jacques de Loutherbourg (1740-1812).

Coal had of course been shipped for centuries down the east coast of England to London and the rural south. The ease of transporting goods around the coast and the relatively short distance of all places in Britain from the sea, had always been a major advantage for trade. By the start of the French Revolutionary War in 1793, this was supplemented by a system of canals that linked almost every centre of heavy industry to navigable rivers and the sea. Communication by land was also fast compared to that in many continental countries. Between 1750 and 1790 some 1,600 Acts of Parliament were passed to extend and improve turnpikes, whose proprietors came to control over 24,500 miles of road in Britain.

TRADE AND EMPIRE

During this period there was a remarkable growth in foreign as well as domestic trade. Traffic with Europe, once a main source of Britain's imported wealth, had long since been overtaken by trans-oceanic trade with the East and with North America. The value of imports by the East India Company rose sixfold during Nelson's lifetime and those from the West Indies fourfold. Trade with North America had fallen disastrously during the War of Independence, but it recovered and developed with unexpected strength after 1783, quadrupling between 1784 and 1804. At the same time, the Baltic trade tripled in size, a reflection of the vast quantity of naval stores it supplied for the con-

Wealth through trade: an East India Company convoy returning home in 1802, led by Captain George Millet as commodore in the Hindustan. From a painting by Nicholas Pocock (1740-1821).

struction and maintenance of both the Royal Navy and the merchant fleet. Such was the momentum of foreign trade growth in this period that it continued despite interference from war, a phenomenon unknown before the mid-eighteenth century.

Colonies, according to the economic wisdom of the day, went with trade. They existed to provide the mother country with a favourable balance of trade, a profit held in gold and silver to pay for its army and navy in times of war. The wars of the period therefore aimed to dispossess other European powers of their colonial sources of wealth. At the same time, explorers attempted to discover new colonies and trade routes. The explorations of Captain Cook would have been well-known to Nelson from his childhood and early naval career. He himself went on Captain Phipps's expedition in 1773 to seek a north-east passage into the Pacific (see page 67). He no doubt shared the sense of national loss when the American colonies made good their independence in 1783. The remarkable regeneration of trade which followed this, however, disproved the traditional mercantile theory of colonies and, over the next half century, began to vindicate the new 'free trade' ideas of Adam Smith. Meanwhile Nelson attempted to maintain the laws derived from the traditional theory. In the West Indies between 1784 and 1787 he tried to prevent the Americans, now outside the British system, from trading directly with British colonies, to the fury of the influential colonists who benefitted from evading their own government's regulations (see page 73).

REVOLUTIONS AND THE NAVY

Though proud of his professional ability to execute the orders of his superiors as he understood

K1, Larcum Kendall's official copy of Harrison's perfected H4 chronometer of 1759, was used by Cook on his second and third voyages. He proved its accuracy and came to rely on it.

them, Nelson none the less imbibed the innovatory spirit of the age. The Navy, no less than Britain itself, was affected by political, economic, technological and social change; and, just like the philosophers, thinking naval officers were developing new theories for using their resources.

After the disastrous outcome of the American War, the political consideration most affecting the Royal Navy was its realization that failure to defeat an enemy fleet decisively could have dire consequences. Revolutionary France used armies ideologically committed to total war — 'the Republic or death'. To defeat French fleets and defend Britain against invasion, the commitment of the Royal Navy also had to be total. The British fleet was prepared for this: between 1783 and 1793 it was completely rebuilt. It was perhaps appropriate that Sir Charles Middleton, who presided over this reconstruction, should become First Lord of the Admiralty in 1805 in time to co-ordinate the campaign which led to Trafalgar. He was at the Admiralty as First Sea Lord in

CAPTAIN COOK

The three Pacific voyages undertaken by Captain James Cook from 1768 to his death on Hawaii in 1779, largely completed the picture of the world begun by the Portuguese and Spanish discoveries of the fifteenth century. His navigation was greatly helped by John Harrison's development of a practicable marine chronometer or 'sea-watch' and his work as a chart maker set unprecedented standards of accuracy. Nelson's navy benefitted from such improvements, though the Admiralty Hydrographic Office was only established in 1795 and official French charts remained generally the best into the early nineteenth century. Cook's discoveries in the Pacific, which seemed like an earthly paradise, also had great influence on scientific and cultural thought.

ABOVE *Cook's ships* Resolution *and* Adventure *in Matavai Bay, Tahiti, in about 1773; by William Hodges (1744-97).*

RIGHT *Captain James Cook (1728-79) by Hodges, official artist on Cook's second voyage in 1772-5.*

ABOVE *Trade protection: John Paul Jones captures His Majesty's ships* Serapis *and* Countess of Scarborough *off Flamborough in 1779, during the American War. This was a triumph for the young American navy but Captain Pearson of the* Serapis *was knighted for successfully defending his valuable Baltic convoy, all of which escaped. Engraving by Robert Dodd.*

LEFT *'Sailors, the Republic or Death', reads this French boarding flag taken in Lord Howe's victory of the Glorious First of June, 1794.*

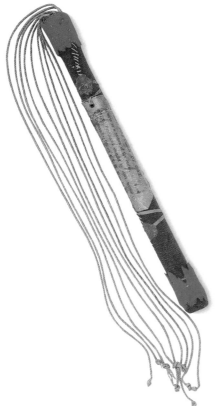

'The Point of Honor'. A seaman, bound to an upended deck grating, is about to be flogged when the real defaulter owns up. A marine guard is drawn up on the poop above. By George Cruikshank, 1825.

Cat-o'-nine-tails: an official mid-nineteenth century pattern. Flogging was already in decline at that time and was stopped in 1879.

Charles Middleton, Lord Barham, Admiral of the Red (1726-1813). He succeeded Nelson's uncle as Comptroller of the Navy under Lord Sandwich and was First Lord of the Admiralty, 1805-6. Artist unknown.

1794–5 when it was decided that an Inspector General of Naval Works, an officer specifically commissioned to make technological improvements in the Navy, should be appointed. Middleton was also an evangelical in his religious opinions and interested in promoting humanity in the forms of punishment employed in the Navy. It was no coincidence that his administration was followed by the prohibition of 'starting' (hitting seamen with a rope's end or cane to hurry them on) and of punishment by running the gauntlet. Middleton thus acted as a medium through whom many of the reforming forces bearing on the Navy were translated into changes in its management.

Nelson played a similar role at sea. He was able to take advantage of such new techniques as ramming guns with flexible rope rammers and firing them with a flintlock, and the signalling system using a numeric symbolism of flags.

He also built on the understanding, inherited from successful earlier commanders, that the enemy line had to be broken and a pell–mell battle achieved (previously breakthrough had been only partial and engagements limited to sections of the combattant fleets). As he mastered the management of a fleet at sea, Nelson developed tactics capable of totally annihilating the enemy. This, together with his charismatic and generally humane personal qualities as a leader, confirmed his role as an agent of profound change in the Navy. In a professional sense he was a complete man of his time, making his own contribution to the Age of Revolutions.

C H A P T E R

NELSON'S NAVY

FROM the beginning of the eighteenth century, the British Navy was the largest force of its kind in the world. When Nelson was two years old in 1760, it had 412 ships; when he died in 1805, it had 949. All these were, of course, powered by the wind, though some of the smaller craft could also be rowed. Vessels of any size – ships of the line, frigates and most sloops – were ship-rigged: that is, they had three masts, all carrying square sails. Nelson is chiefly associated with the biggest ships in the fleet, the ships of the line, so-called because they were large enough to stand in the line of battle, where each might engage an opponent of roughly equal size. These were the ships which won Nelson's great battles and in which he sailed from 1793 onwards, following the outbreak of war with Revolutionary France.

THE SHIPS

The largest ships of all were the great three-deckers, each with three complete decks of guns. They were divided into two main groups, the First Rates with 100 guns or more, and the Second Rates which had 90 or 98. The differences of rate do not sound very significant, but the Second Rates generally had lighter guns, so their force was considerably less. The most famous of the First Rates was the *Victory*, which carried 104 guns at the time of Trafalgar. She was

VICTORY

MONUMENT TO AN AGE

The *Victory* was already a famous and popular flagship when Nelson was a junior officer. A First-Rate, 100-gun three-decker, she was designed by Sir Thomas Slade and floated out at Chatham Dockyard in 1765. Measuring 186ft (57.25m) on the gundeck and of 2,162 tons, her armament varied over the years but at Trafalgar was thirty 32-pounder guns on the lower deck, twenty-eight 24-pounders on the middle deck, thirty 12-pounders on the upper deck and twelve 12-pounders on the quarterdeck; she also had two 12-pounders and two 68-pounder carronades on the forecastle. In all, a broadside weight of 1,148lbs of shot. She first saw action in 1778, during the American Revolutionary War and was Jervis's flagship at Cape St Vincent in 1797. Substantially rebuilt in 1800-3, she was last used at sea as flagship in the Baltic in 1812. She then remained afloat on harbour duties at Portsmouth until moved into permanent dry-dock there in January 1922, for restoration to her Trafalgar condition. *Victory* is still the flagship of the Commander-in-Chief, Naval Home Forces, the world's oldest serving warship and the only surviving line-of-battle ship.

ABOVE *24-pounder guns on the middle gundeck.*

ABOVE *The original open stern galleries were enclosed during the 1800 rebuild. From top to bottom they belong to the captain's cabin, the 'great' or admiral's cabin and the wardroom.*

RIGHT *Model of Victory's original figurehead. It was replaced by a smaller one of the Hanoverian royal arms during her pre-Trafalgar rebuild.*

LEFT *Nelson's day cabin.*

Bellona, *a classic 74-gun, two-decker Third Rate. She was built in 1760 and served with Nelson at Copenhagen in 1801. This original model, on launching ways, was probably commissioned in the 1770s to demonstrate the process of coppering to George III. '74s' made up more than half Nelson's fleet at Trafalgar.*

a well-regarded ship but was forty years old and rather old-fashioned by this time. Recently built First Rates had 110 guns and several with 120 guns were under construction; the French and Spanish had used ships of this size for some years.

The three-deckers served as strong points in the fleet and added prestige but in many ways the two-deckers were more important. They sailed better and were more economical of scarce resources such as timber and men. The most important was the 74-gun ship, which had been the most common type of ship of the line since the 1760s. When Admiral the Earl of St Vincent chose a fast and effective squadron for Nelson to re-enter the Mediterranean in 1798, he gave him 74-gun ships and it was these which won the Battle of the Nile (see page 92). According to a leading naval architect of the time, the '74' was the ideal compromise:

Of those that carry [their guns] *upon two decks, the 74 gun ship is the most approved …. The 74 gun ship contains the properties of the first rate and the frigate. She will not shrink from an encounter with a first rate on account of superior weight, nor abandon the chase of a frigate on account of swiftness. The union of these qualities has therefore, with justice, made the 74 gun ship the object of maritime attention, and given her so distinguished a pre-eminence in our line of battle.*[1]

Also classed as Third Rates, along with the 74s, were ships of 80 and 64 guns. 80-gun ships were quite rare and their numbers were mostly made up by captures from the French. The 64 was quite a common type. Nelson enjoyed his service in the 64-gun *Agamemnon*, from 1793; the ship had 'the character of sailing most remarkably well'.[2] However, there were many who believed that the 64 was too small to serve in a modern line of battle. 'There is no difference of opinion respecting the 64 gun ships being struck out of the rates. It is a fact that our naval officers either

pray or swear against being appointed to serve on board them.'[3] In addition, there were still some Fourth-Rate ships of two decks and around 50 guns in the fleet. These were even less effective as ships of the line than the 64s and too slow to serve as frigates. However, the 50-gun *Leander* served under Nelson with some distinction at the Battle of the Nile.

Next in size and status below the ships of the line were the frigates. Each of these carried its main armament on a single deck, with a raised quarterdeck and forecastle. There was a lower deck, as on a ship of the line, but it was unarmed and largely below the waterline. Nelson commanded frigates in America and the West Indies

The 32-gun frigate Triton, *built (unusually, of fir) at Deptford in 1796 and here shown hove-to. Nelson never had enough of these ships 'Was I to die this moment,' he wrote after the Battle of the Nile, '"Want of frigates" would be found stamped on my heart.' By Nicholas Pocock.*

in the early stages of his career. He later bemoaned the lack of them to provide reconnaissance forces for his fleets, especially during the Nile campaign. Frigates usually had 32 or 36 guns and were of the Fifth Rate. Sixth Rates had between 20 and 28 guns and were sometimes regarded as small frigates. Yet smaller were the sloops of 18 guns or less. These could carry out many of the tasks of the frigate, such as convoy escort, but they were unsuitable for fleet reconnaissance as they could not fight off the enemy frigate screen.

There were numerous smaller vessels in the fleet. Brigs were two-masted and square-rigged and were slightly smaller versions of the sloop.

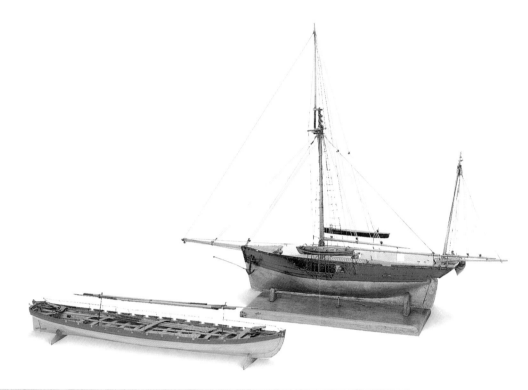

Models of a ship's launch (1:48), the largest working boat carried on board, and the naval yawl Entreprenante *(1:108).*

The 14-gun hired armed cutter Telemachus *with her captain John Crispo, in the full-dress of a commander. This picture of 1797 perhaps marks his promotion from lieutenant, in which rank he commanded* Telemachus *when she took two French privateers off the Isle of Wight in August 1796. Artist unknown.*

Cutters and schooners were fore-and-aft rigged, so could sail closer to the wind. They were largely used for carrying messages and for patrol; it was the schooner *Pickle* which brought the news of Trafalgar, and Nelson's death, to England. Bomb vessels were among the most specialized in the fleet. Each was designed round a pair of mortars, used to bombard an enemy fortress or town. There were seven in Nelson's squadron at Copenhagen. Fireships were often conversions of old merchant vessels. Filled with combustible materials, they could be set alight and put on a course towards the enemy. They were relatively easy to avoid and few were used in Nelson's time. The smallest vessels in the fleet were rowing gunboats, used for inshore work against invasion at home, and in narrow waters such as at Gibraltar and around Denmark.

The fighting fleet was supported by many other vessels. In port it was attended by harbour craft; sheer hulks – essentially floating cranes – were used to lift the masts into ships, while other hulks were used for storage, or to accommodate seamen awaiting allocation to crews. At sea,

A sea cook, often a man disabled as shown. This and the following prints of naval personnel are from a set by Thomas Rowlandson, 1799.

A purser.

LEFT *A sheer hulk at work in Portsmouth harbour. From a print after John Cleveley jnr, 1772.*

A carpenter.

A captain of marines.

transport craft for troops, ammunition and naval stores were mostly hired from merchant shipowners.

During the eighteenth century it was commonly believed that the French built much better ships than the British. The most successful types, such as the 74 and the frigate, had certainly been developed by the French during a particularly creative period in the 1730s and 1740s. Captain Edward Brenton was echoing a widespread opinion when he claimed that 'the ships of France and Spain were generally superior to those of England, both in size, weight of metal, and number of men, outsailing them in fleets, and often in single ships, carrying their guns higher out of the water, and in all respects better found in the material of war.'[4] The founders of the Society for the Improvement of Naval Architecture were also convinced of 'the inferiority of our warships as compared with those of France and Spain'.[5]

French ships were popular with naval officers because of their alleged good sailing but modern research shows that this was best achieved in light wind conditions. British ships were more robust and able to stand heavier weather. This difference reflects the naval strategies of the two nations. The French spent most of their time in port, ready to make a quick dash to a specific objective. The British believed in sea power for its own sake; they waited outside the French ports, usually well to seaward, and their ships had to be able to cope with any conditions.

The negative reputation of British ships dated largely from the first half of the eighteenth century, when ship design had indeed been very backward. By the 1780s the British were being more innovative. They were the first to use copper sheathing on the underwater hulls of their ships. This produced great advantages in the later years of the American War, preventing fouling by weed and barnacles which drastically reduced a ship's efficiency, and protecting against structural attack by shipworm. The British also developed a short, powerful gun known as the carronade, which was to prove very effective in the close-range battles fought by Nelson and his contemporaries. The quality of British rope had been much improved by Joseph Huddart's invention of a new method of laying strands and hundreds of smaller inventions were tried. Claims by frustrated inventors that the Royal Navy was slow to adopt technical change were a distortion of the truth.

Ships for the Navy were built both in the Royal Dockyards and in privately owned shipyards. The dockyards were concentrated in the south of England, with Deptford and Woolwich on the Thames, Chatham and Sheerness on the Medway, and Plymouth and Portsmouth on the south coast. Naval shipbuilding in private yards also took place mainly in these areas, so that it could be done under the supervision of Royal

Chatham Dockyard, about 1792, by Joseph Farington (1747-1821). Victory was built in the Old Single Dock, third from the right, from lines laid out in the Mast House and Mould Loft above the docks on the left. The dock and Mast House survive, with most of the brick buildings shown here.
INSET
The Chatham Mast House of 1753 as it is today.

Dockyard officials. The shipbuilding industry of north-east England, for example, was little used for naval purposes.

The dockyards also maintained the ships, using dry-docks to inspect and repair the underwater hulls. Each yard contained vast stocks of timber, canvas, tar, rope and other naval stores. The western or forward dockyards, Plymouth and Portsmouth (those closest to the main French naval base at Brest), each formed the centre of a naval base, with an ordnance depot, marine barracks, naval hospital and victualling yard and with anchorages close by where a fleet or convoy could be assembled or await a favourable wind to enter port.

THE OFFICERS

The Navy had two types of officer. Sea officers were the only commissioned ranks, apart from Royal Marine officers. They commanded the ships and fleets and provided the lieutenants who were the watchkeeping and administrative

captain under whom they happened to serve. The sea officers were the only people trained entirely within the naval service, normally from the age of about twelve or thirteen. There was a Naval Academy at Portsmouth but it provided only a small proportion of officers; the majority had all their training afloat. Most boys intended for sea-officer status served about three years rated as able seamen or captain's servants, before being promoted to midshipmen and given a share in the responsibility for running the ship: taking charge of one of the boats, becoming second-in-command of a watch, commanding a group of guns in action or supervising the welfare of a group of seamen.

After six years' service, a midshipman could present himself for examination for lieutenant. The examination was conducted orally before three captains and the level of difficulty varied. Some candidates were passed on the nod but Sir Charles Middleton, for example, prepared a rigorous set of questions:

Your ship being now under courses [the lower sails of each mast]*, you are supposed to be in such a situation as to oblige you to wear; give the proper orders, and wear your ship.*

An enemy is observed; give orders for clearing your ship, and make the necessary preparations for engaging.[6]

Having passed the examination, the candidate was not always promoted immediately. There was often a surplus of eligible young men and he might have to spend some time as a 'passed midshipman' before being commissioned as a lieutenant. There were 3,104 lieutenants in the Navy in 1812. Some commanded small vessels, such as gunboats. Most served on the larger ships, taking charge of a watch on a ship of the line or a frigate. Each had responsibility for a 'division' of the crew, looking after their welfare and health. In action he would command some

officers. The warrant officers were 'trade specialists', not normally eligible to command ships, or even to take charge of a watch in most cases. They included the master, purser, surgeon, chaplain, boatswain, carpenter and gunner of each ship; also more junior grades such as the master-at-arms, cooper and cook. Thus they covered a great social range, from the cook of a sloop to the Physician of the Fleet. They were all appointed by warrant from the Admiralty, however, so that their status did not depend on the whims of the

Sir Thomas Masterman Hardy (1769-1839), as a captain in about 1801. A Dorset man who became Nelson's protégé, friend and longest serving flag-captain, a role he filled almost continuously from 1799 to Trafalgar, where he commanded Victory. Artist unknown.

of the ship's guns, perhaps half a deck. There was no formal specialization but the senior or first lieutenant on each ship was in charge of its administration and had no watchkeeping duties.

Nelson's navy was too large for the Admiralty to know each officer personally, and there was no system by which individual performance was reported to it. To be promoted, a lieutenant had to attract the notice of either the Admiralty in home waters, or the commander-in-chief on an overseas station. One way to do this was through 'interest', the influence of a family connection perhaps, or a political favour by (or owed to) his relatives at home. Nelson's early promotion sprang partly from his uncle being Comptroller of the Navy, although by then his own great abilities were also becoming evident. The system might seem corrupt and inefficient to modern eyes but on the whole it worked. Incompetents were rarely promoted far because their lack of ability could not be concealed in a man-of-war and represented a real danger.

For those who lacked 'interest', the other way to rise was through merit, often measured by fighting success. It was the custom to promote the first lieutenant of a ship which distinguished itself, either in a fleet battle or a single-ship action. After all of Nelson's victories, for example, the surviving senior lieutenant of each ship was promoted to commander or even captain. Nevertheless, hundreds of lieutenants failed to attract the notice of authority and never got beyond that rank.

A commander was in effect a junior captain, who would take charge of an unrated vessel such as a sloop as 'master and commander'. From this position, some were rapidly promoted to 'post' captain. Others had to remain commanders, largely because there were too many of that rank and it was difficult to find an opportunity to

distinguish oneself further. Having been 'made post', an officer's career was largely assured. He would probably be captain of a frigate in the first instance, then of increasingly large ships of the line. He might serve as commodore, as Nelson did at the Battle of Cape St Vincent. This rank was a temporary one, conferred for specific duties, but gave him authority over other captains. After about fifteen or twenty years he would, by seniority alone, reach the head of the captains' list and be promoted to Rear-Admiral of the Blue, if he was to remain active, or made a 'yellow admiral' if he was to be retired.

Promotion for admirals was also by seniority and still reflected the way the fleet had been organized to fight the Dutch in the 1660s. There were three basic ranks: rear-admiral, vice-admiral and admiral, with each divided into three squadrons known as the red, white and blue, in descending order of seniority. Thus a Rear-Admiral of the Blue would be promoted to Rear-Admiral of the White, while a Rear-Admiral of the Red's next step was to Vice-Admiral of the Blue, and so on. Until the 1740s there had been only one officer in each rank but in the 1790s there were about two hundred admirals. There was no Admiral of the Red at this period; only one officer at a time had this seniority and was known simply as the Admiral of the Fleet.

The warrant officers were vital to the Navy and often as important as the junior lieutenants. The most important of all was the master, who was responsible for the navigation of his ship, in the broadest sense. As well as determining its position and setting courses, he was expected to take control during a difficult manoeuvre, such as tacking in confined waters. He was also responsible for the stowage of the hold and had several assistants, known as master's mates, who were usually senior midshipmen awaiting promotion.

The importance of the surgeon is obvious. He had to be medically qualified (though the status of a surgeon was much lower than that of a physician) and to have served a certain number of years at sea, according to the rate of his ship. Surgeons were hard to find in the 1790s because of poor pay and conditions but the situation was improved by pay rises in 1794 and 1805. The surgeon was assisted by the number of mates appropriate to his ship, all medically qualified. The purser was the ship's supply officer but his role was partly that of a private sub-contractor. He was paid less than equivalent officers and had to give substantial securities on his appointment. He was expected to make a personal profit on many of his transactions and it is no surprise that he was often accused of cheating the crew. Chaplains were rare aboard ship before their conditions were improved in 1812. A chaplain entering the service before then soon found that 'nothing can possibly be more unsuitably or more awkwardly situated than a clergyman in a ship of war'.[7]

Surgeon's medicine chest belonging to Sir Benjamin Outram KCB, used at the Battle of Copenhagen in 1801.

Sir William Beatty (c.1770-1842), a physician who also acted as surgeon of Victory *during the Trafalgar campaign and attended the dying Nelson. He wears physician's full-dress uniform of 1803-25. By Arthur William Devis (1763-1822), about 1806.*

Silk hangings from Nelson's cot, partly embroidered by Lady Hamilton.

A midshipmen's berth in a British frigate in about 1822, by Augustus Earle (1793-1838). An unusual composite view of 'mids'' leisure-time activities and possessions, though the quarters were not as generous as this suggests. A marine is coming up from below.

All these officers had use of the wardroom, while the master's and surgeon's mates berthed with the midshipmen. The other three main warrant officers, the gunner, carpenter and boatswain, lived mainly in their own cabins and were regarded as being of lower social status. They were known as 'standing officers', because they stayed with the ship even when the crew changed or the ship was out of commission. They were responsible for maintenance of, respectively, the guns and ammunition, the hull and masts, and the rigging. The boatswain was also responsible for mustering the crew: his mates roused them from sleep and wielded the cat-o'-nine-tails during punishment.

Nearly all the officers lived at the stern of the ship. On a ship of the line, the captain had a moderately large cabin on the quarterdeck, with an open stern gallery on most of the older vessels. On a three-decker, the admiral's cabin was immediately below and slightly larger; on a two-decker this was omitted. Aft, on the middle deck of a three-decker, or the upper deck of a two-decker, was the wardroom. This was shared by the lieutenants, marine officers and principal warrant officers. It was:

about 35ft in length, and 16 or 18ft wide. Within the walls, which are of painted canvas, are the cabins of six officers; the centre of the room is occupied by a mess table; and the extremity, under the stern windows, by a projection called the rudder head. The opposite end is arranged as to do the office of a side board; with the door of entrance on one side of it; and space to sling a quarter cask of wine on the other [8].

The gunroom, aft on the lower deck, was less comfortable: the tiller was mounted above and it was difficult to sling hammocks. Small cabins for the junior marine officers, the chaplain or the pilot, were fitted in the corners, while the rest of the space was used as a schoolroom for the ship's boys, or as an office for the clerks. The cockpit was below, under the waterline in the bowels of the ship. Round the sides were store rooms and cabins for the purser and surgeon. The rest of the space was allocated to the midshipmen, with a communal berth for them on each side. On a ship of the line of the early 1800s, one of these was described as 'twenty feet long, with a table in the middle of it, and wooden seats upon which we sit ... there are fourteen of us in the mess at the same time'.[9]

NAVAL RECRUITMENT

The press-gang was perhaps the most notorious aspect of the Navy in Nelson's time. According to popular legend, the gang roamed the streets, terrorizing honest citizens and dragging them off

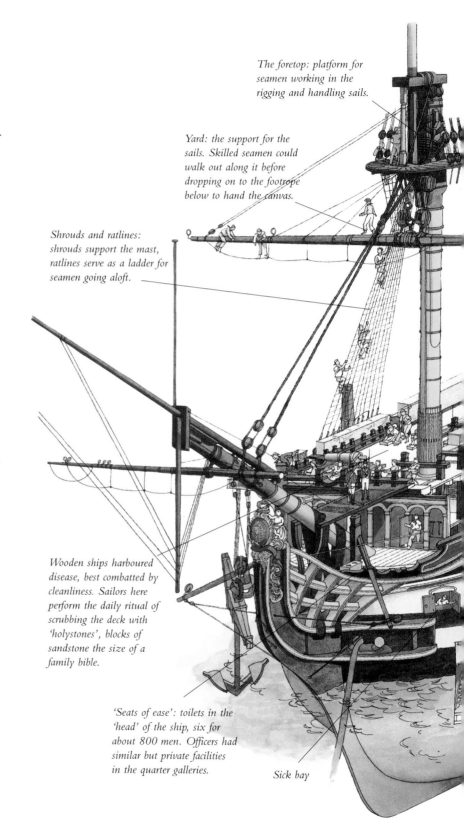

The foretop: platform for seamen working in the rigging and handling sails.

Yard: the support for the sails. Skilled seamen could walk out along it before dropping on to the footrope below to hand the canvas.

Shrouds and ratlines: shrouds support the mast, ratlines serve as a ladder for seamen going aloft.

Wooden ships harboured disease, best combatted by cleanliness. Sailors here perform the daily ritual of scrubbing the deck with 'holystones', blocks of sandstone the size of a family bible.

'Seats of ease': toilets in the 'head' of the ship, six for about 800 men. Officers had similar but private facilities in the quarter galleries.

Sick bay

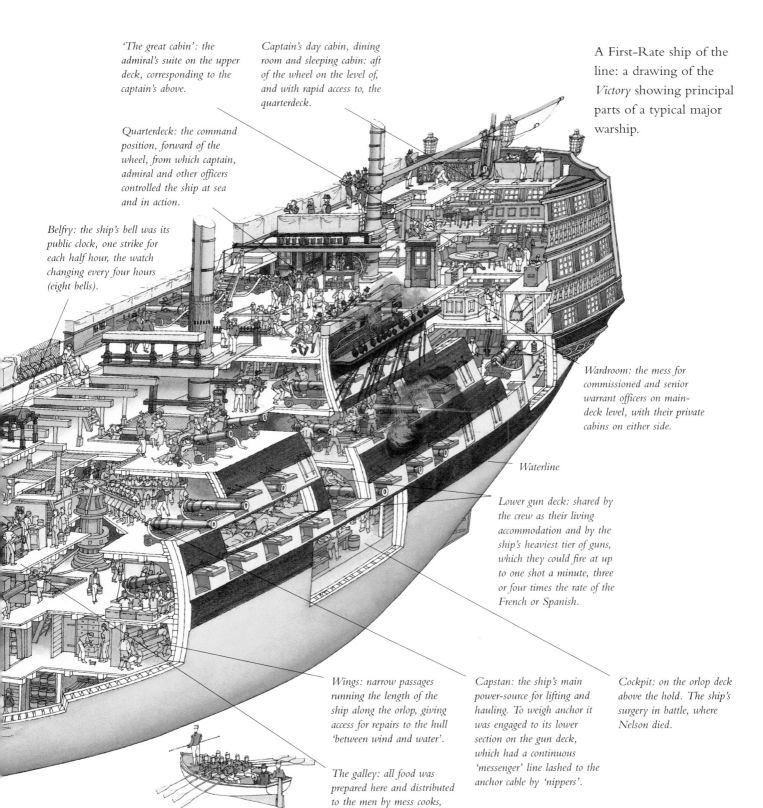

'The great cabin': the admiral's suite on the upper deck, corresponding to the captain's above.

Captain's day cabin, dining room and sleeping cabin: aft of the wheel on the level of, and with rapid access to, the quarterdeck.

A First-Rate ship of the line: a drawing of the *Victory* showing principal parts of a typical major warship.

Quarterdeck: the command position, forward of the wheel, from which captain, admiral and other officers controlled the ship at sea and in action.

Belfry: the ship's bell was its public clock, one strike for each half hour, the watch changing every four hours (eight bells).

Wardroom: the mess for commissioned and senior warrant officers on main-deck level, with their private cabins on either side.

Waterline

Lower gun deck: shared by the crew as their living accommodation and by the ship's heaviest tier of guns, which they could fire at up to one shot a minute, three or four times the rate of the French or Spanish.

Wings: narrow passages running the length of the ship along the orlop, giving access for repairs to the hull 'between wind and water'.

Capstan: the ship's main power-source for lifting and hauling. To weigh anchor it was engaged to its lower section on the gun deck, which had a continuous 'messenger' line lashed to the anchor cable by 'nippers'.

Cockpit: on the orlop deck above the hold. The ship's surgery in battle, where Nelson died.

The galley: all food was prepared here and distributed to the men by mess cooks, who collected and shared it out among their messmates.

A sleeping cabin on the Gloucester, 74 guns, in 1812: chaplain Edward Mangin's in fact but similar to other officers', as is the hanging cot. The window looks forward along the main deck.

Dinner in the wardroom of the Gloucester. Though crude, it shows the officers' cabins on each side. Both these views are by Edward Mangin.

unwillingly to serve in atrocious conditions. Certainly the gangs did use violence and provoked counter-attack. In 1803, for example, the impress officer at Sunderland told his superior that 'he durst not attempt to impress at that place last night, as mobs of hundreds of seamen, soldiers and women, got round the rendezvous and threatened the lives of his people, whether they acted or not'.[10] There were also occasions when all and sundry were taken by the press. At Harwich during the general 'hot press' on the resumption of war in 1803:

The market house was to be their prison, where a lieutenant was stationed with a guard of marines, and before daylight next morning their prison was full of all denominations, from the parish priest to the farmer in his frock and wooden shoes. Even the poor blacksmith, cobbler, tailor, barber, baker, fisherman and doctor were dragged from their homes.[11]

Such events were exceptional, if only because

the men needed for such raids could not often be spared from their naval duties. Moreover, only experienced seamen were liable to impressment; others had to be released as soon as they could

LEFT *Nelson's cabin washstand, a common item of furniture among naval officers. Other designs doubled as a dressing table and desk.*

RIGHT *Leather-covered armchair from Nelson's cabin furniture.*

establish their identity. At the same time as the Harwich affair, Admiral Lord Keith had to apologise to the Mayor of Margate:

On such an occasion as a general impress, it is morally impossible to carry the orders of the government into execution without incurring some risk of seizing upon individuals who are not liable to be impressed .... Captain Byng has already discharged such of the men as he thought could not be legally detained.[12]

At other times, pressing was on a much reduced level. The regular work was carried out by the shore-based impress service, which in 1795 included eighty-five gangs around the country, each consisting of about eight men led by a lieutenant.[13] On a more individual basis, a warship short of its complement would land a gang to make up the deficiency. Impressment also took place at sea and ships could wait in the Channel or in anchorages such as the Downs to take seamen from homecoming merchantmen. Men were also recruited by other means. Some were volunteers, often lured by large bounties. Some were raised under the Quota Acts of 1795, whereby each local authority had to supply a fixed number of men for the Navy. A large proportion of landsmen of dubious character entered the Navy in this way and may have contributed to the mutinies of 1797.

According to one seaman, 'the dread of a ship of war was next to a French prison'.[14] The work was certainly hard and the food often poor, but these factors varied from ship to ship and, on average, there is no reason to believe that they were worse than in the merchant service. Pay was also poor but was not much less than it was in the peacetime merchant fleet. In war, however, the pay of merchant seamen rose rapidly because of their scarcity, while those forced into the Navy could no longer share in this sudden wealth. Most of all, seamen feared the Navy because there was no official way out until peace returned, perhaps in eight or ten years time. On being impressed in 1794 the seaman John Nicol wrote, 'I found myself in a situation I could not leave, a bondage that had been imposed on me against my will, with no hopes of relief until the end of the war.'[15]

'Manning the Navy': the London press-gang and its victims caricatured in a print of 1790. The area round the Tower of London was full of seamen from vessels in the Pool and the impress service consigned those it took to a receiving ship moored there.

THE SEAMAN

The object of all this recruitment effort, and one of the main foundations of British naval power, was the seaman. He was regarded – not least by himself – as a separate race, or almost a separate species. He had his own style of dress, his own vocabulary and even a different way of walking. He could run up the rigging in a storm to take in sail, man the guns in action, steer the ship, perform dozens of knots, hitches and splices, and all other duties of shipboard life. But it was attitude,

ATTIC MISCELLANY.

Drawn by Collings.   Publish'd as the Act directs by Bentley & Co June 1,st 1790.   Etch'd by Barlow.

MANNING THE NAVY.

ABOVE 'The Jolly Tars of Old England on a Land Cruise', 1802. Seamen's fun ashore – commandeering a stagecoach and terrorizing landlubbers. A print after J. C. Ibbetson.

ABOVE 1804 recruitment poster for the frigate Pallas, 36 guns, captained by the dashing Lord Cochrane. Captains with a reputation for taking rich prizes could largely man their ships from volunteers.

RIGHT A bosun's mate of the Gloucester, pictured in his best shore-going rig by Edward Mangin, 1812. The ship's name on his tarpaulin hat is forerunner of the modern naval 'cap tally', but the dress is not an official uniform.

rather than skills, which made the true seaman so valuable:

It is only men of such description that could undergo the fatigues and perils of sea life; there seems to be a necessity for being inured to it from an early age. The mind, by custom and example, is thus trained to brave the fury of the elements in their different forms, with a degree of contempt at danger and death that is to be met with nowhere else, and which has become proverbial. Excluded by the employment which they have chosen from all society but people of similar dispositions, the deficiencies of education are not felt, and information on general affairs seldom courted. Their pride consists in being reputed a thorough bred seaman, and they look upon all landmen as beings of an inferior order .... Fine clothes for his girl, a silver watch, and silver buckles for himself are often the sole return for years of labour and hardship. When his officer happens to refuse him leave to go on shore, his purse is sometimes with the coldest indifference consigned to the deep, that it may no longer remind him of pleasures he cannot command.[16]

Seamen of the French Wars found much to complain of in conditions of service and had two main ways in which to express this: by desertion and by mutiny. Desertion was endemic in the days of the press-gang and every captain had to take it into account when authorizing shore-leave. According to Nelson, 42,000 men deserted during the French Revolutionary War (1793-1801), and Admiral Philip Patton claimed that 12,000 men 'ran' in the two years after the conflict resumed in 1803. It was certainly not cowardice that caused seamen to desert and they never did so in the face of danger. More likely it was a sense of injustice against being confined aboard ship while others were able to make good money in the merchant service or enjoy the pleasures of the shore.

Naval mutiny became more common after about 1783, when the crew of the *Janus* locked their officers in their cabins. It culminated in 1797, when the fleets at Spithead, off Portsmouth, and the Nore, off Sheerness, mutinied in succession. The Spithead affair was successful for the seamen: they were given their first pay rise in nearly 150 years and an improvement in conditions. The Nore mutiny was much more bitter. The mutineers were eventually isolated and their leaders, including Richard Parker, were hanged.

Sailors Carousing in the Long Room at Portsmouth. *Tavern 'long rooms' were for general entertainments. Here seamen spend arrears of pay and prize-money on drink and women, and play conkers with watches. By Julius Caesar Ibbetson (1759-1817).*

These fleet mutinies were essentially naval strikes, non-violent and with limited aims. Small-ship mutinies were rather different. They often occurred far at sea and saw the ship's officers deposed or even killed, with the result that the mutineers became fugitives from their native land. The most famous, of course, was the *Bounty* mutiny of 1789. Her commander, Lieutenant Bligh (who, as a captain, later served bravely under Nelson at Copenhagen), was cast adrift in an open boat and the mutineers' leaders eventu-

ally found refuge on remote Pitcairn Island. Much more violent was the *Hermione* mutiny of 1797. This began when the brutal Captain Pigot ordered that the last men off the yardarm be flogged, provoking a stampede in which two men died. That night the crew rose, killed most of the officers and surrendered the ship to the Spanish.

Nelson was never personally involved in a mutiny. In 1797 he was under the Earl of St Vincent in the Mediterranean fleet and by spring 1798, when the spirit of mutiny had spread

The cutting out of the Hermione *from Porto Cabello, Venezuela, 24 October 1799. Boats of the* Surprise, *Captain Edward Hamilton, went in at night to retake the* Hermione *from under Spanish guns two years after she was handed over by the mutineers who killed her officers. By Nicholas Pocock.*

south, he had begun the detached service which would lead to the Battle of the Nile. In the meantime, St Vincent ruthlessly suppressed all signs of rebellion. When a man was hanged for mutiny, St Vincent often insisted that the crew of the condemned man's own ship carry out the deed:

Each ship of the squadron is to send two boats with an officer in each, and two marines or soldiers properly armed in the stern sheets of each boat, on board His Majesty's ship St George at half past seven o'clock

John Jervis, Earl of St Vincent, Admiral of the Fleet (1735-1823). Nelson's formidable superior served with Wolfe at Quebec in 1759 and through the American War, before commanding the Mediterranean and Channel Fleets during the French Wars. He was a reforming disciplinarian with a grim sense of humour, though less successful as First Lord of Admiralty, 1801-5. By Sir William Beechey.

tomorrow morning (Sunday) to attend a punishment. The sentence is to be carried into execution by the crew of the St George alone, and no part of the boats' crews of other ships as is usual on similar occasions, is to assist in this painful service, in order to mark the high sense the commander in chief entertains of the loyalty, fidelity and subordination of the rest of the fleet.[17]

There is evidence that Nelson's punishment rate was as high as anyone else's but his charis-matic leadership undoubtedly had great effect on the men under his command. When he flew his flag in the *Theseus* in 1797, the ship's company had recently arrived from England and was much affected by the spirit of mutiny. Nelson brought in his own officers and transformed the crew's attitude: 'Success attend Admiral Nelson!', they wrote. 'God bless Captain Miller! We thank them for the officers they have placed over us. We are happy and comfortable, and will shed every drop of blood in our veins to support them, and the name of the *Theseus* will be immortalised as high as the *Captain's* [Nelson's ship at the Battle of Cape St Vincent].'[18]

THE REST OF THE CREW

Royal Marines formed about 30 per cent of the fleet in wartime, though for part of the French Revolutionary War not enough could be recruited. Soldiers were sent aboard to fill their place, which they did with some distinction. Marines were recruited without any sea experience and were trained as soldiers in the barracks at the main Royal Dockyards. The great majority were assigned as shipboard detachments, forming part of the crews of virtually all naval vessels of about 10 guns or more. They had their own commissioned officers, with sergeants and corporals like

'Saturday Night at Sea.' George Cruikshank's print shows relaxation round a mess table suspended between the guns. The men sit on sea-chests with their mess utensils and bags of personal kit on the bulwark behind.

the army. In addition to their fighting roles as marksmen and in amphibious warfare, the marines provided an armed and disciplined force against insurrection by the seamen. This was particularly so in St Vincent's fleet in 1798, as is shown by the orders issued to his captains:

Whenever there is occasion to inflict punishment on board any of His Majesty's ships under my command, the respective captains are hereby required and directed to cause an officer's guard of marines to attend the punishment, with loaded arms and bayonets fixed, in the manner it has been practised on board the Ville de Paris; and inform themselves from Lt. Col. Flight how the guard is paraded and drawn up preparatory to, and during the punishment. When at anchor in this position, the whole party of marines in the respective ships of the fleet is to be kept constantly at drill or parade under the direction of the commanding officer of marines, and not to be diverted therefrom by any of the

ordinary duties of the ship. Sighting the anchors or getting under sail are the only exceptions which occur to the commander in chief.[19]

Apart from the seamen themselves, numerous skilled workers were needed to keep a ship operational. The complement of a 74 included 10 carpenter's crew, who would work under the carpenter on the maintenance of the hull, masts and boats. There would be an armourer and two mates, who were the ship's skilled metal-workers, as well as sailmakers, coopers and caulkers. There were many servants, working in the captain's cabin, wardroom, gunroom and midshipmen's berth. Some servants were boys, others were adults. The rest of the crew was made up of landsmen – adults who had no sea experience. They would spend their time hauling on ropes, scrubbing decks and assisting the seamen in their various tasks. A few of the younger ones would go aloft and eventually become real seamen but

'A True British Tar', 1795. *The public image of the sailor used by Gillray to lampoon Nelson's naval friend Prince William Henry, Duke of Clarence. 'Jordan' – slang for chamber-pot – is a coarse pun on the name of his mistress, Mrs Jordan.*

BELOW 'Equity or a Sailor's Prayer before Battle. Anecdote of the Battle of Trafalgar.' *'Why Starboard! How is this at prayers when the enemy is bearing down upon us; are you afraid of them?' 'Afraid - No! I was only praying that the enemy's shot may be distributed in the same proportion as the prize money, the greatest part among the Officers.' William Heath's comment on naval inequalities, 1805.*

A TRUE BRITISH TAR.

most, especially those older than about twenty-five, had no real hope of advancement.

SEAMANSHIP

Without wind, ships of the line could not move at all, except with very great effort by the ships' boats. Frigates and sloops had some provision for rowing but it was rarely used. Except in an emergency or a chase, ships and fleets tended to wait for a favourable breeze or planned their routes to take likely winds into account.

The Colour of Admirals. The flags tell the story in this view of a fleet coming to anchor, painted by Peter Monamy in the 1740s. The Commander-in-Chief, the Admiral of the Fleet, with the pre-1801 Union flag at the main, is making the signal to anchor - the striped ensign flying astern of his First-Rate three-decker flagship. Under his command he has a vice-admiral of the red squadron, flying a plain red flag on his foremast, and a rear-admiral of the blue, with a blue flag on the mizzen. The ensigns of the ships in their divisions are red and blue respectively. Nelson's last rank was Vice-Admiral of the White, one step below the vice-admiral shown here, and flew white, always a St George's cross, at the fore (see page 27). A full admiral would wear the colour of his squadron on the mainmast. After 1747 captains promoted to half-pay rear-admiral, and in effect retired, were informally known as the 'yellow' squadron.

The Glorious First of June, 1794. *Lord Howe's flagship*
Queen Charlotte *(left) has just broken the French line astern*
of their flagship Montagne *(right). She failed to close action as*
shown here, through loss of the fore-topmast, but the brilliant
seamanship of James Bowen, Howe's sailing master, earned
him a commission and he rose to be an admiral.
By Philippe-Jacques de Loutherbourg.

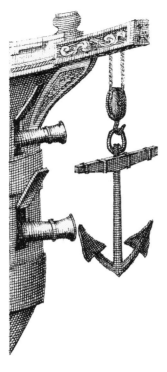

A bower (i.e. bow) anchor suspended at a cathead.

135. In ideal conditions a ship of the line or frigate might reach 13 or 14 knots (sea miles per hour), but 5 or 6 knots was far more usual. Average speeds were difficult to calculate, as a good run on one day might be followed by flat calm. Strong winds were not necessarily an advantage, as a captain would have to take in sail for safety, while rough seas could also impede progress. Conversely, if the winds were very light, the captain might order studding sails to be set. These were extensions to the width of the normal sails, which might add enough speed for the rudder to become effective. In action, a ship normally carried a minimum of sail as men had to be called from the gun crews to tend it. Despite the light winds at Trafalgar, Nelson did not set studding sails to speed his approach to battle.

It was risky for a large part of the fleet to enter an enclosed port together, as it might be some time before a favourable wind allowed them to get out again. As a result, ships spent much time

All ships of any force were square-rigged. They sailed well with the wind coming from astern, less well into the wind. A square-rigged ship could sail in 20 out of 32 points of the compass; that is, it was unable to sail closer than about 67½ degrees towards the direction from which the wind was blowing. If forced to go upwind, the ship would follow a zig-zag course known as tacking, or beating to windward. It would sail as close to the wind as possible on one tack, and then turn to repeat the procedure on the other. The turn could be done in two ways: by pointing the ship's bows up through the wind (also known as tacking) or by turning the stern to the wind, known as wearing. Tacking ship required considerable skill, suitable wind and sea conditions and the combined efforts of a large part of the crew, since all the sails had to be altered at exactly the right moment. Wearing ship was easier but required a good deal of space and lost a certain amount of time and leeway as the ship turned through some 225 degrees rather than

'Heaving the lead' *by John Augustus Atkinson, 1808. An able seaman in the fore chains taking soundings.*

in open anchorages such as Spithead, and at Torbay, Devon. Anchors were therefore very important, not to say essential when a ship was being driven on shore and in many other circumstances. Ships usually carried four main anchors, including two spares. They also had two smaller ones which could be slung under boats, then rowed ahead and dropped, providing an emergency means of towing. Anchor cables were made of very thick rope and were 120 fathoms long (720 feet/221.5 metres).

Dropping an anchor was relatively simple but raising it involved the whole crew. Dozens of men (usually the marines) pushed at the capstan

Quarter-scale model of a 68-pounder carronade on a naval slide carriage, as fitted on the lower deck of the Second Rate Royal William in 1782. Invented in 1752 and made from 1778 by the Carron ironworks, Scotland, these guns were adopted by the Navy in the 1780s with 12-, 24- and 32-pounder being common sizes. A 32-pounder could be worked by three or four men. Short-range weapons, they were called 'smashers' owing to their effect.

bars to provide the main force. A team of skilled seamen stood by on the forecastle. When the anchor broke surface, they caught its ring and raised it to the cathead, a projection from the bows of the ship. Another team 'fished the anchor' and it was stowed so that it would not knock against the ship's side. More men were stationed below, coiling the cable so that the water could drain out of it. The topmen, the skilled and active seamen of the crew who worked up the masts amid sails and rigging, were already aloft, ready to release the sails for the ship to get under way.

WEIGHT OF METAL

The main armament of warships in the 1790s was still the cast-iron, muzzle-loading 'long' gun, of which the heaviest in general British use was the 32-pounder (shot weight) requiring a minimum crew of seven or eight men. However, in the early 1780s the Navy had also adopted the 'carronade', a light, short-range gun capable of being handled by under half the men for the same weight of shot. This was solid iron ball against hulls and heavy spars; bar and chain shot against rigging and men, and grape-shot specifically to kill men. The main gunpowder charge was pre-loaded in paper or cloth cartridges both for safety and convenience of use. Battles took place quite literally in a 'fog of war', rapidly generated by the dense white smoke of burning powder.

ABOVE *This 40lb shot was fired into the bow timber of* Victory *at Trafalgar from the huge Spanish four-decker* Santissima Trinidad. *The whole section was cut out and preserved.*

RIGHT *Double-headed bar shot fired at* Victory *from the* Santissima Trinidad *at Trafalgar. This killed a file of eight Marines on the deck and was preserved by their lieutenant, Lewis Rotely.*

BELOW *Flintlock for cannon: invented by Captain Sir Charles Douglas in the American War, this version dates to 1819.*

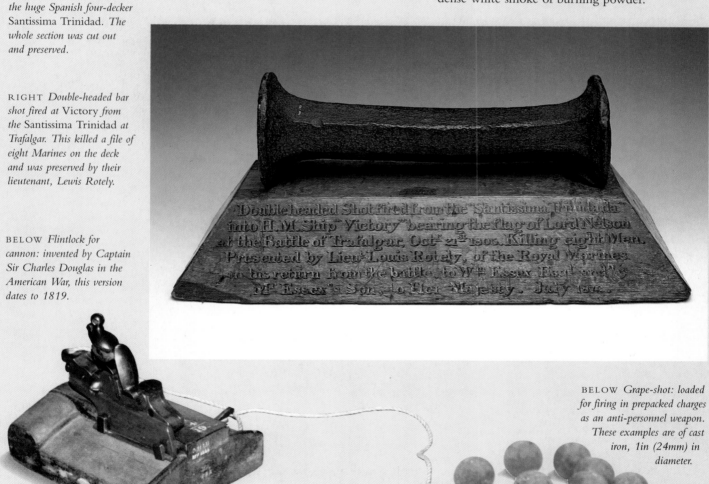

BELOW *Grape-shot: loaded for firing in prepacked charges as an anti-personnel weapon. These examples are of cast iron, 1in (24mm) in diameter.*

The guns were the prime *raison d'être* of a warship and in action the main task of the crew was to load, aim and fire them. The gun itself was little more than a long cast-iron tube closed at one end. To load it, a powder cartridge and shot were rammed down the barrel from the muzzle end. By this time, in British ships, firing at the touch hole was normally by a flintlock, like that of a musket, which gave almost instant discharge. The gun then recoiled and was reloaded before being hauled back so that its muzzle again projected through the gunport. This was the heaviest work of all and involved the whole gun crew, about fifteen men in the case of a 32-pounder on the lower deck of a ship of the line.

The bore of the gun was smooth and its effective range only a few hundred yards. The most common shot was solid iron, which stood some chance of penetrating thick wooden hulls. Explosive shells were not used at sea, except in

ABOVE *Brodie patent galley stove or firehearth, about 1780. Most food for the large numbers of seamen was boiled in the stove's coppers, but it could also roast and bake. Seamen always ate before battle, when the stove was put out to reduce risk of fire. This is a manufacturer's model by George Cawthorn of Rotherhithe.*

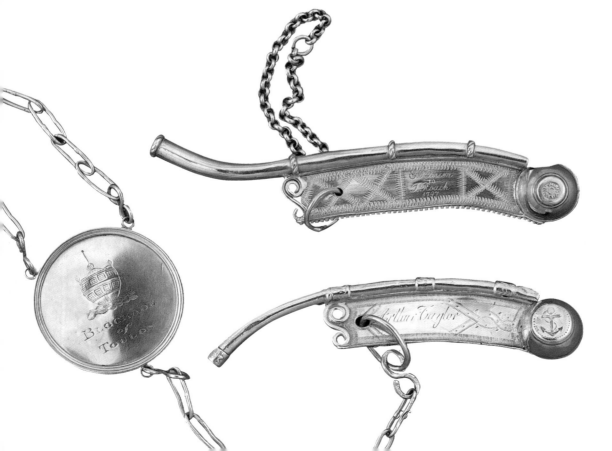

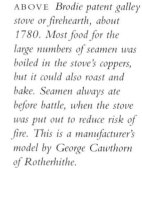

LEFT *Silver bosun's calls. The various 'pipes' made from these whistles transmitted a range of standard shipboard orders. That above was used at the Battle of Camperdown in 1797, the one below at the blockade of Toulon, 1810, which the medallion commemorates.*

Hard tack. Ship's biscuit was made of flour and water slowly baked. This one was given as a souvenir to a Miss Blacket of Berwick in 1784.

bomb vessels' mortars for shore bombardment, but alternative ammunition might include chain-shot, for use against rigging, or grape-shot against personnel. British crews prided themselves on their rate of fire rather than accuracy and may have been able to achieve one round per minute. This does much to explain Nelson's dictum that 'no captain can do very wrong if he places his ship alongside that of an enemy.'[20]

SHIPBOARD LIFE

A 100-gun ship like the *Victory* had a crew of over 800 men, a 74 had around 600 and even a frigate needed 200 to 300. To get the best use of the men, they had to be divided into teams for many different purposes. For fighting, the quarter bill was drawn up. This divided the men into crews for each of the guns, with others to steer, use the small arms, handle the sails and provide ammunition from the magazines. In normal times, daily routine was covered by the watch bills. Some men, especially those involved in

maintenance, were given day-work and could usually enjoy a full night's sleep. The rest were divided into watches, one of which was always on duty when the ship was at sea. Most ships had two watches, though a few had three. A watch was also a period of time, normally four hours, so seamen on a two-watch ship at sea would be working four hours on, four hours off. Each watch was also sub-divided, according to the parts of the ship in which the men worked. Thus a 74-gun ship would have 25 fore-topmen to a watch, 27 main-topmen and 15 mizzen-topmen. There were 25 forecastle men, who worked in the fore part of the ship with anchors and other equipment. These tended to be older seamen, less capable of going aloft. The 22 men of the afterguard, and 6 of the poop afterguard, were less skilled but worked on the quarterdeck, directly under the eyes of the officers; for this, smarter men were likely to be chosen. The least desirable men tended to become 'waisters', working in the central part of the ship on the most menial duties. The rest of the crew was made up of marines (who also stood watch); petty officers such as quartermasters, boatswain's mates and the gunner's crew; signalmen, boys, servants and tradesmen, such as coopers and carpenters. Many of these worked only in the daytime and were therefore known as 'idlers' to their shipmates.

To anyone but an experienced seaman, life on the lower deck of a warship was one of extreme hardship. A ship needed a large crew to man its guns and had to spend long periods at sea, so the men were crammed into a small space. The lower deck of a ship of the line was home for perhaps 500 men, fitted in between 28 or 30 large guns. Men slept in hammocks, with 14 inches (35cm) width allowed to each man, except for petty officers who had 28 inches. One benefit of using the two-watch system at sea was that both watches' accommodation could be interspersed, giving each man twice the allocated sleeping space. The atmosphere could be fetid:

On the same deck with me, when the crew was complete, slept between five and six hundred men; and the ports being necessarily closed from evening to morning, the heat in this cavern only six feet high, and so entirely filled with human bodies, was overpowering.[21]

The seamen also ate on the lower deck. They were divided into messes and in a ship of the line set up tables between each pair of guns. Food was very basic; meat such as pork or beef four days a week, with cheese, peas and ship's biscuits on the other days. Fresh vegetables were purchased when available from the shore, as their importance in preventing scurvy was now understood. The meat was boiled by the ship's cook, who had his galley stove under the forecastle. Mealtimes were quite long, often an hour and a half for dinner, at midday. Captains often insisted that the whole crew should eat together, except for a few helmsmen and lookouts, and they were 'never to be interrupted at their meals but on the most pressing occasions, and the commanding officer should be very punctual as to their hours of dinner and breakfast'.[22] At mealtimes discipline was relaxed and the crew had a short period of leisure. They were allowed to choose their own messmates to a certain extent and could enjoy spending time with their friends.

MEDICINE

In view of the hardships of sea life, the long periods without shore contact and the speed with which disease could spread in a crowded vessel, the importance of nautical medicine cannot be overestimated. Its greatest achievement in Nelson's lifetime was the conquest of scurvy through the issue of fresh vegetables, lime and lemon juice. This allowed the fleet to carry out

John Ross, a seaman who lost a leg at the Nile, sits beside Nelson's servant Tom Allen, who holds the admiral's portrait. Allen, also from Burnham Thorpe, served with Nelson from 1793 but missed Trafalgar. Detail from watercolour by S.P. Denning, after John Burnet's oil of Greenwich Pensioners on Trafalgar Day 1835, painted for the Duke of Wellington.

long blockades and gave Nelson a relative independence of shore bases during his campaigns. From 1801, each ship of the line was fitted with a sick berth under the forecastle, where there was good ventilation but also heat from the galley stove when required. In action, the after cockpit, home of the midshipmen and some distance below the waterline, was transformed into an operating theatre for the surgeon and his mates. It was in the cockpit of the *Vanguard* that Nelson was treated when injured at the Nile, and in the cockpit of the *Victory* that he died at Trafalgar.

In the days before anaesthetics, any kind of delicate operation was almost impossible and surgeons specialized in swift amputation. The cockpit in action was a scene of horror, as the wounded were brought down from the battle above: *Ninety wounded were brought down during the action. The whole cockpit deck, cabins, wing berths and part of the cable tier, together with my platform and my preparations for dressing were covered with them.... Melancholy calls for assistance were addressed to me from every side by wounded and dying, and piteous moaning and bewailing from pain and despair. In the midst of these agonizing scenes, I was able to preserve myself firm and collected, and embracing in my mind the whole of the situation, to direct my attention where the greatest and most essential services could be performed.*[23]

OTHER NAVIES

One of the key factors in Nelson's success was his precise judgement of his enemies' capabilities. All

The horrors of sea war: a remarkable although unfinished picture of the Battle of the Nile, 1798, emphasizing the human costs of a major action. The ship on the right may be the French Tonnant, *whose captain lost both arms and a leg but continued to direct action supported in a barrel of bran until he died. In the background the French flagship* L'Orient *blows up. By Mather Brown (1761-1831).*

his campaigns were against opponents of similar technology and culture (apart from the revolutionary tendencies of the French and Americans), so it is relatively easy to compare one navy with another.

Nelson never encountered the United States navy after it was revived in the 1790s for punitive operations against Barbary corsairs. It had fine frigates, with very capable officers and crews, at a time when the British were scraping the barrel as far as both timber and men were concerned. Seven years after Nelson's death the Americans gave the British a shock in a series of frigate actions during the brief Anglo-American War of 1812. The United States navy was the only one which could compare with Britain's, ship for ship, but fortunately for Nelson's successors it was too small to have more than an effect on morale.

The French navy was much larger, the second largest in the world after the British. Its ships were of fine quality, though not as superior as some British officers claimed. The crews were reasonably competent, though France had a smaller number of seamen on which to call. Its system of conscription, the *Inscription Maritime*, was never as efficient in practice as it was on paper but it was a great advance on the British press-gang. France, however, suffered from a lack of well-placed naval harbours and had no large base on its Channel coast from which to launch an invasion of Britain.

The French navy's biggest problems were political. With a vulnerable north-eastern frontier, France always set greatest defensive store on her army: the navy was definitely the second service. This was exacerbated when a landsman such as Napoleon held the reins of power and consistently failed to understand the limits and practicalities of naval conflict. Because of its inferiority in numbers, the French navy's strategy was to put to sea only for specific expeditions. This of course meant that the ships were clean and in good shape and contributed to the myth of French shipbuilding superiority; but it also meant that their crews lacked training, especially in the vital matter of gunnery.

The second problem was the state of the officer corps. The French navy contributed significantly to Britain's overall failure in the American War, considering itself victorious when this ended in 1783. However, its officer structure was dominated by the aristocracy, many of whom died, fled or lay low during the French Revolution. The new government attempted to fill the gap with political commissars, rapidly promoted petty officers or merchant captains, but none of these provided an effective substitute for a professional officer corps. The French navy was thus totally disrupted in the early stages of the war and was only beginning to recover its self-esteem when Nelson changed the picture again

Red and gold battle ensign of the Spanish San Ildefonso, *captured at Trafalgar, hanging from the Queen's House, Greenwich, in 1962. The flag (below) has the emblems of Castile and Leon in the centre and measures 50 x 32ft (15.25 x 8.9m).*

with his crushing victory at the Nile in 1798. That battle, with St Vincent's policy of keeping the French fleet in port by continuous blockade, ensured that its officers would not regain their effectiveness. Their defeat at Trafalgar was the final blow.

Spain had the next largest navy. Its shipbuilding policy oscillated between copying the British and copying the French. Partly as a result of this synthesis, it produced some very fine vessels. It specialized in very large ones, such as the four-decker *Santissima Trinidad* which Nelson attacked at Cape St Vincent and eventually captured at Trafalgar. Spanish officers were brave and generally skilled seamen, having taken part in many transatlantic voyages to their own colonies. Like the French, they lacked experience in fleet manoeuvres and tactics and this was to prove their downfall in their two great battles against the British off Capes St Vincent and Trafalgar. As regards seamen, the Spanish had an even smaller base than the French from which to recruit their navy. Large numbers of landsmen had to be used, and there was never enough sea-time to train them into effectiveness.

The Dutch navy came next in size, with a long-standing and creditable history of fighting the Royal Navy in the North Sea, most recently in the American War. It again became a threat when Revolutionary France invaded the country in 1793, was welcomed by the population, and set up the Batavian Republic there two years later. As the historic 'United Provinces', the Dutch actually had several different navies: each of the maritime provinces had its own fleet, not always completely compatible with the others, though all shared a strong seafaring tradition and a large merchant marine from which to draw seamen. The officers often had links with the merchant service, which meant that they tended to think of getting safely from port to port rather than engaging the enemy, but as a whole the Dutch were good fighters. The biggest problem was their ships, which were restricted in size by the shallowness of their home waters. They had no three-deckers at this time and only a few 74-gun ships. The majority of their ships of the line were 64s, regarded as obsolete in other navies. Nelson never encountered the Dutch but they were decisively defeated by Admiral Duncan off Camperdown, on the Dutch coast, in 1797.

Vice-Admiral Pierre-Charles de Villeneuve (1763-1806) narrowly avoided capture at the Nile in 1798, when his flagship Guillaume Tell *was one of only two major French vessels to escape. He commanded the Franco-Spanish Combined Fleet at Trafalgar, was captured there with his flagship* Bucentaure, *and died by suicide on his return to France the following year. A print after Edme Quenedey (1756-1830).*

The Danish navy also took up both British and French ideas, producing a few innovative ships. Like most navies, it used 74s, and was fairly effective until beaten to a standstill off its home port of Copenhagen by Nelson in 1801. The Swedish navy, too, was quite original in its ship design and employed Frederick Af-Chapman, a Swedish naval architect of international reputation, to devise gunboats for inshore defence. Of other navies, Venice and Austro-Hungary had locally effective forces in the Adriatic, while Russia's navy was strong in numbers of ships but very weak in quality and organization. Nelson came into direct contact with the last after the Nile, when Russia's 'mad Czar' Paul allied himself briefly with Turkey and Britain and Nelson had to deal diplomatically with both their Mediterranean squadrons. His opinion of neither was high, though he preferred Turkish 'natural sense' and willingness to co-operate to the suspicious jealousy of the Russians: 'The Russian Admiral [Ouschakoff] has a polished outside but the bear is close to the skin [24]....As for the Turks, we can do anything with them. They are a good people, but perfectly useless.'[25]

'THE MEREST BOY':
NELSON'S EARLY CAREER, 1758–94

RIGAUD'S early portrait of Nelson, finished in 1781 when he was twenty-three, shows a spare, fine-boned and sensitive youth. Nelson's height – about five feet, six inches (158cm) – was not notably short for his day but he remained slight and, in the hundreds of later images made during his life and within living memory of him, he is commonly shown as small compared to others. Throughout his naval career his undoubtedly serious wounds and a succession of illnesses, amplified by a tendency to hypochondria, seemed to confirm his physical frailty.

A description of Nelson by HRH Prince William Henry, written in 1782, just after Rigaud delivered this portrait, suggests that the artist suppressed his subject's customarily eccentric appearance:

Captain Nelson appeared to be the merest boy of a captain I ever beheld and his dress was worthy of attention. He had on a full-laced uniform: his lank, unpowdered hair was tied in a stiff Hessian tail of extraordinary length; the old-fashioned flaps on his waistcoat added to the general appearance of quaintness of his figure and produced an appearance which particularly attracted my notice, for I had never seen anything like it before, nor could imagine who he was, nor what he came about.[1]

That this apparently frail and odd young man should become the greatest admiral the Western world has ever known, has always proved a puzzle. How could he survive the shocks and hardships of prolonged life at sea to win three major battles and, by doing so, change the course of European history? There are several answers to this. Firstly, despite appearances, Nelson's constitution was not frail. When he died, a post-mortem on his body by *Victory*'s surgeon,

Nelson as a captain, by John Francis Rigaud (1742-1810). Begun in 1777 when he was a lieutenant but finished in 1781, for his friend and commander Captain Locker. The background commemorates his part in the San Juan river expedition.

William Beatty, revealed him to be in good health: his heart, liver and other vital organs were strong and showed no sign of disease; indeed, according to Beatty, they were more like those of a youth than a man of forty-seven.

ABOVE Nelson asks Dr Gaskin of the Society for Promoting Christian Knowledge for bibles and prayerbooks for his 500-man crew. Written with his right hand while fitting the Agamemnon for sea at Chatham, March 1793. He made similar requests for his later commands.

Nelson's left-hand writing, from the only letter (to Admiral Kingsmill) in which he lists all his wounds, in 1804. After gaining his Sicilian dukedom, he tried several signatures before settling on 'Nelson & Bronte'.

Secondly, Nelson's eccentricity concealed an intellect and ambition that distinguished him from others. On being introduced to him in 1782, Prince William Henry also noticed 'something irresistibly pleasing in his address and conversation and an enthusiasm when speaking on professional subjects that showed he was no common being'.[2] In September 1805 the future Duke of Wellington – nearly eleven years younger than Nelson and only just beginning his rise to fame – had a similar experience, while waiting in the Colonial Office to see Lord Castlereagh, the Secretary of State. Nelson, within six weeks of Trafalgar and his death, came in on similar business and, not recognizing him, engaged the aristocratic young general in conversation. Wellington found the little admiral's talk 'so silly as to surprise and almost disgust'; it was almost a monologue and all about himself. Wellington then made some comment which prompted Nelson to leave the room and find out who he was. He returned 'altogether a different man, both in manner and matter'. All that Wellington had thought 'a charlatan style' had vanished:

he talked of the state of this country, and of the aspect and probability of affairs on the Continent with a good sense and a knowledge of subjects at home and abroad that surprised me... in fact he talked like an officer and a statesman. The Secretary of State kept us long waiting, and certainly, for the last half or three-quarters of an hour, I don't know that I ever had a conversation that interested me more.[3]

The experience of others was similar. Beneath his surface vanities, Nelson had a grasp and enthusiasm for current affairs that few could rival. Alexander Scott, *Victory*'s chaplain, called him 'the most fascinating companion I ever conversed with... interesting beyond all, on shore, in public and even in private life'.[4]

Nelson's birthplace. The parsonage house at Burnham Thorpe, Norfolk, was an L-shaped building, formerly two big cottages. Bitterly cold in winter, it was pulled down three years before Trafalgar. By Francis Pocock.

The best testimony to Nelson's determination is his career. From his very earliest days, he was known for his spirit and resolution. Within his own family, his small stature counted for nothing. Deputed to stop a fight between him and his bigger, bullying brother, their sister apparently retorted: 'Let them alone, little Horace will beat him'. Other anecdotes tell of the boy pushing on to catch a coach through deep snowdrifts, although his older brother wanted to return; and of Nelson carrying out a plan to raid the head-master's orchard, while all his fellow pupils were deterred by fear of the punishment if caught. On one occasion he said to his grandmother, 'I never saw fear; what is it?'

ENTRY INTO THE NAVY

It was no accident that this small but spirited dare-devil joined the Navy. Although Nelson was only the son of a country rector, the Reverend Edmund Nelson of Burnham Thorpe in Norfolk, his mother Catherine was the sister of a successful naval captain, Maurice Suckling. Both, in turn, were children of a Prebendary of Westminster and related to the influential Walpole family. Maurice had fought successfully in the Seven Years War (1756–63). He was recalled to sea at the time of the Falkland Islands crisis of 1770, being appointed to the 64-gun *Raisonnable*, a French ship captured in 1758, the year of Nelson's birth.

Captain Maurice Suckling (1725-78), Nelson's maternal uncle and patron. From a portrait after Thomas Bardwell.

In 1770 Nelson was twelve years old and his aptitudes were becoming clear. His mother had died in December 1767, aged forty-two, leaving Edmund Nelson with five sons and three daughters to care for, educate and place in suitable employment. Through Uncle Maurice, the Navy offered a strong prospect of employment for at least one son. For people like the Nelsons, geographically isolated but with professional expectations, patronage through family connection was the route for sons to enter the forces, the church or the law. It also helped their further progress, depending on the continuing influence of their patrons. To Nelson, the appointment of Suckling to the *Raisonnable* seemed an opportunity too good to miss. His father was away in Bath but he urged his older brother to write and ask Edmund

to press his interest on Suckling. The captain responded positively, though hinting wryly at the hardship and dangers involved:

What has poor Horace done, who is so weak, that he, above all the rest, should be sent to rough it out at sea? But let him come and the first time we go into action a cannon-ball may knock off his head and provide for him at once.[5]

From 1 January 1771, Nelson's name was consequently entered in the books of the *Raisonnable* as a midshipman, but he did not join the ship immediately as she was still a hulk, a ship 'in Ordinary' or reserve, lying in the River Medway at Chatham. He returned for the new term to the Paston School, North Walsham, which he had attended since the death of his mother. Prior to that he had boarded at the Royal Grammar School in Norwich; he thus had a good education for his time and had been accustomed to living away from home in a regime which included harsh corporal punishment. The experience was of value to him in adapting to the Navy, although nothing could fully prepare a boy for the initial shock of life in a ship of war.

Nelson joined the *Raisonnable* in March 1771, on a day when the grey waters of the Medway were swept by fresh gales, squalls and snow. The next few weeks were spent bringing aboard the guns, provisions and equipment, and twice he saw a man punished by flogging at the grating. When the ship eventually dropped down river to Sheerness, the Falklands crisis had been settled. Suckling transferred to the *Triumph*, a guardship at the Nore, off Sheerness, and Nelson followed him. Guardship experience was not likely to help make him a seaman, however, so Suckling arranged for his nephew to join one of his old friends, John Rathbone, who now commanded a West Indiaman about to sail from London for the

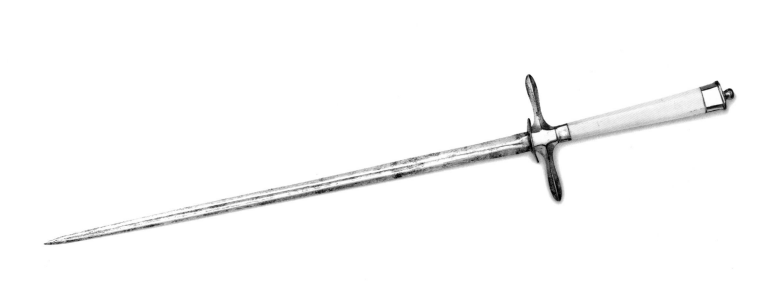

Caribbean. This experience was to form Nelson, not only as a seaman but as someone who could relate to them. He experienced the gulf that divided working men from officers and the merchant service from the Navy as he later recorded: *if I did not improve in my education, I returned a practical seaman, with a horror of the Royal Navy, and with a saying, then constant with the seamen, Aft the most honour, forward the better man! It was many weeks before I got in the least reconciled to a man-of-war, so deep was the prejudice rooted; and what pains were taken to instil the erroneous principle in a young mind!* [6]

THE MIDSHIPMAN

Nelson returned to Suckling and *Triumph* at the Nore, in July 1772. There, the only means his uncle had to promote seamanship in his young men was in command of the ship's cutter and long-boat. Nelson was able to learn how to handle such small craft and to navigate shallow waters without mishap:

Midshipmen wore dirks rather than swords; this one dates to 1775, is 16in (40.5cm) long overall and was supplied by Banks of Plymouth Dock.

Thus by degrees I became a good pilot for vessels of that description from Chatham to the Tower of London, down to the Swin, and to the North Foreland; and confident of myself amongst rocks and sands, which has many times since been of the very greatest comfort to me. [7]

As Nelson grew more confident and competent, he needed to widen his experience, as Suckling was well aware. Yet in peacetime, with the minimum number of ships in commission, opportunities were all too few. In 1773 Suckling was nevertheless able to use his friendship with Lord Sandwich, then First Lord of the Admiralty, to have Nelson considered by Captain Lutwidge for a petty officer's position in the *Carcass*, bomb vessel. This was fitting at Sheerness as an exploration ship to go to the Arctic with the *Racehorse* in an attempt to find a north-east passage into the Pacific. Nelson, still only fourteen, was able to convince Lutwidge to take him as his coxswain, a tribute to his earnest enthusiasm and ability, to which Suckling would also have testified.

Nelson transferred to the *Carcass* in May 1773 and with numerous other adventurous and inquiring minds experienced the challenges of polar exploration. At fourteen it is hard to be responsible at all times and his impetuosity gave rise to one hare-brained, night-time attempt to kill a polar bear. Otherwise his energy and enthusiasm soon gained his officers' approval. The expedition pushed up the west coast of Spitzbergen and Nelson applied his experience in small boats to navigating through the ice.

Nelson and the Bear. *Nelson wanted a polar bear's skin for his father but his musket misfired when he made an unauthorized sortie to shoot one. Fortunately a crack in the ice stopped the bear ending a promising midshipman's career and it was frightened off by a shot from the* Carcass. *By Richard Westall (1765-1836), for Nelson's 1809 biography.*

Towards the end of the brief summer, apparently trapped by floes and encroaching ice, it seemed they might have to abandon the ships. Nelson was pleased, then, to be given command of a four-oared cutter with 12 men, for he prided himself that he could navigate that vessel better than any other boat in the ship. Through these means he gained the friendship of the expedition's leader, Captain the Hon. Constantine Phipps, later Lord Mulgrave, another important connection of Lord Sandwich.

Engraved for PAYNES Universal Geography.

Vol. V. page 481.

View of the RACEHORSE and CARCASS August 7th 1773, when inclosed in the ICE in Lat. 80°.37' N

The expedition was paid off in the Thames on 15 October 1773. Good reports to Sandwich and Suckling quickly secured Nelson a new berth in the frigate *Seahorse,* commanded by Captain George Farmer, who had been one of Suckling's midshipmen during the Seven Years War. He was to serve in her for two years, cruising on the East Indies station between the Persian Gulf and the Straits of Malacca. Eventually malaria brought him low and he returned in the *Dolphin,* which paid off at Woolwich on 24 September 1776.

It was on this voyage home that Nelson had a spiritual, quasi-religious experience, which he

Racehorse and Carcass in the ice, August 1773. Both ships were nearly trapped in their search for a north-east passage through the Arctic. Engraving after John Cleveley jnr, based on sketches by Midshipman Philippe d'Auvergne.

later described and which has always been considered significant in his development. Weakened by illness and despondent about future promotion prospects, he was unexpectedly inspired by a 'radiant orb'. A sudden glow of patriotism was kindled within him and he visualized his king and country as his patrons. 'Well then,' he determined, 'I will be a hero and, confiding in Providence, I will brave every danger!'[8] For Nelson, then approaching eighteen years of age and in a weakened physical and psychological state, it was an experience that reinforced his ambition and resolve.

LIEUTENANT NELSON

Through his connection with Sandwich, Suckling had now become Comptroller of the Navy; that is, chairman of the Navy Board which, under the Board of Admiralty, managed the dockyards, shipbuilding and other practical aspects of the service. Suckling's influence had thus increased, with prompt consequences for his nephew's career. Only two days after the *Dolphin* paid off, Nelson received an order from the Commander-in-Chief at Portsmouth to become an acting-lieutenant of the 64-gun *Worcester*. The thirteen British colonies in America had declared their independence on 4 July and were now receiving encouragement from France, so the winter of 1776–7 saw the *Worcester* escorting convoys and patrolling the North Sea. It was a toughening experience from which Nelson emerged with increased confidence in his ability to manage a ship. On 9 April 1777 he was examined for lieutenant in London. In theory, he should have reached twenty years of age and he was not yet nineteen. The examination was chaired by his uncle who gave no sign of recognition and only revealed the family connection after Nelson passed. He received a commission the next day as second lieutenant of the 32-gun frigate *Lowestoffe*, bound for the West Indies.

For two more years Nelson was to receive the attention that went with Suckling's powerful patronage. He became the close friend of William Locker, captain of the *Lowestoffe*, and took command of the schooner that was adopted as her tender. He learned to navigate in the Caribbean islands and captured his first prize. Then, when Sir Peter Parker came out to assume command on the station early in 1778, he took Nelson into his flagship, the *Bristol*, as third lieutenant. As prizes were taken and commands became available it was the practice for the senior

Captain William Locker (1731-1800), Nelson's captain in the Lowestoffe. *They became friends and Nelson stayed with Locker in 1797 when he was Lieutenant-Governor of Greenwich Hospital, a post he held until his death. By Gilbert Stuart (1755-1828).*

lieutenants to be placed in them. So Nelson rose to be first lieutenant and was then given command of a brig, the *Badger*. It was in the *Badger* that he helped save the crew of the 20-gun warship *Glasgow*, which caught fire in Montego Bay, Jamaica, in May 1779.

THE POST-CAPTAIN

Suckling died in July 1778, having nobly launched his nephew's career, and in July 1779 Nelson was made a post-captain in the 28-gun frigate, *Hinchinbroke*. Before he could take this up, however, Parker put him forward to command one of the harbour-defence batteries at Kingston,

Lieutenant Nelson leaving Captain Locker and the Lowestoffe to take command of a prize, 20 November 1777. The first lieutenant had declined to go, saying conditions were too rough to attempt boarding. Painted in 1806 by Richard Westall for the 1809 biography.

Jamaica, against a threatened French invasion attempt on the island. The attack did not come but the American War was escalating. The French had allied themselves with the American rebels and formally declared war on Britain in 1778. Spain followed suit in June 1779 and, as a result, British attention in the Caribbean now also focused on the Spanish colonies of mainland Central America.

In Jamaica the Governor-General, Major-General John Dalling, had the idea of launching an attack up the San Juan river, which marked the boundary between Nicaragua and Costa Rica. The target was the Spanish inland river fortress, El Castillo de la Immaculada Concepcion. If it could be held by a British army, the Spanish territories in Mexico could be separated from those to the south, and British forces might even be able to enlarge their holding into a potential colony. The plan was well received in London, but Admiral Parker was less enthusiastic, having few vessels to spare for a venture that promised no naval advantage. Nelson, still only twenty-one, was none the less dispatched with the *Hinchinbroke* to escort troopships to the mouth of the river and do whatever else was necessary to forward the expedition. Colonel Polson, who was to command the advance party of troops, recalled him as a 'light-haired boy...of whom I at first made little account.'[9]

Seven troop transports sailed in convoy from Kingston on 3 February 1780, arriving after some delay in the mouth of the San Juan river on 24 March. The military advance up the river began four days later in smaller vessels and canoes. Even before it started, overloading and mishandling of the boats indicated the need for naval assistance. Nelson accordingly volunteered to accompany the expedition, with 50 sailors and marines, in the *Hinchinbroke*'s cutter and pinnace. After a week of

heat, high humidity and tropical jungle, Nelson assisted in the capture of an island outpost of Spanish sentries. On 11 April the expedition reached its goal and laid siege to the fortress. One of the first ashore, Nelson assisted in establishing gun batteries from which he directed the firing. In spite of ammunition shortage and tropical rainfall, preparations were soon ready for an assault. Nelson, however, had felt the first symptoms of dysentery on landing and was now an invalid. Death seemed inevitable if he remained and he was placed in a canoe for rapid descent to the sea, shortly before the fortress fell, late in April.

Back in the *Hinchinbroke*, Nelson transferred command to Cuthbert Collingwood and sailed for Jamaica in a tender to take up a new commission in the *Janus*. He had already received the order for this but his immediate preoccupation was recovery and convalescence. Admiral Parker invited him to use his house, where Nelson

Nelson by Collingwood (left) and Collingwood by Nelson. Drawn in 1785 when both were in the house of Captain John Moutray, commissioner of the naval dockyard at Antigua. The pictures were given to their friend Mrs Moutray.

eventually recognized the need to return to England for a full recovery. He sailed in September, arriving at Portsmouth on 1 December 1780. There he heard the news that the San Juan expedition had been withdrawn, almost all the troops and the *Hinchinbroke*'s men having succumbed to disease.

Nelson convalesced in Bath. At first he was so ill he had 'to be carried to and from bed, with the most excruciating tortures'[10], but after a month only his left arm remained useless and even that recovered by March 1781. He then had time to visit members of his family and return home to Burnham Thorpe. The American War continued, with France, Spain and then Holland allied with the rebels, and in August Nelson was commissioned into the *Albemarle*, another 28-gun frigate. The next year was spent escorting convoys across the North Sea, to and from the Baltic, and then across the Atlantic into the St Lawrence River for Quebec. Growing in experience and confidence, Nelson did not shrink from asserting the claims of the Royal Navy to impress seamen from returning East Indiamen, or to receive a courtesy salute from the Danish fortress at Elsinore. Escort duty made its own demands on the naval captain, for merchant ships were notoriously sluggish in obeying convoy instructions and signals. Off the coast of Massachusetts, Nelson learnt to cope with the prospect of action against a superior French force, a threat he averted by skilfully running the *Albemarle* through shoal waters dangerous to her but impassable to the French.

MAKING A REPUTATION

Growing confidence was accompanied by growing ambition. With his uncle dead, Nelson needed another patron. On active service in wartime, the only way to command the favour and atten-

Samuel, Viscount Hood, Admiral of the Red (1724-1816). Hood saw distinguished service in the American War and was Governor of Greenwich Hospital from 1796 to his death, receiving Nelson's body to lie in state there before the funeral in January 1806. By James Northcote (1746-1831).

tion of a senior officer was through commendable activity. Nelson, however, was to learn that this was insufficient without experience, judgement and discretion. From Quebec he was ordered to New York, where he joined Admiral Lord Hood's command, and from there to the West Indies. The war was now dragging to an end but in March 1782 Nelson was given the opportunity to distinguish himself by driving a small garrison of French troops from a fort on Turk's Island, at the southern end of the Bahamas. With two smaller vessels under his command, as well as the

Albemarle, Nelson attempted a direct assault. It was beaten off with casualties and he had to accept that land targets involved risks and costs which could only be reduced to a minimum through special expertise. He was later to make similar assaults at Tenerife and Boulogne but neither was a success; he never really learnt the lessons of the attack on Turk's Island.

More immediate prospects soon absorbed Nelson's attention. Lord Hood, an old friend of his uncle, selected the *Albemarle* to carry Prince William Henry, later King William IV but then a midshipman in the Navy, on a visit to Havana, Cuba, which was then a Spanish colony. With peace in the offing, the visit was intended to promote goodwill, but it was the proximity of two potential patrons which really enthralled Nelson. He had written earlier:

My situation in Lord Hood's fleet must be in the highest degree flattering to any young man. He treats me as if I was his son and will, I am convinced, give me anything I can ask of him: nor is my situation with Prince William less flattering. Lord Hood was so kind as to tell him (indeed I cannot make use of expressions strong enough to describe what I felt), that if he wished to ask questions relative to naval tactics, I could give him as much information as any officer in the fleet.[11]

Returning to England, the *Albemarle* paid off in July 1783. With the war over, Nelson felt in need of recreation and an opportunity to improve his French. Teaming up that November with an old friend, Captain James Macnamara, he travelled to St Omer in Normandy where he remained until the end of December. He had obviously achieved some standing with the Admiralty for, in spite of many claims for employment from officers on half-pay, Nelson received a new commission for the 28-gun frigate *Boreas* in March 1784. The appointment was a surprise to some, but Nelson felt that reputation

rather than influence was now at work. He responded sharply to his brother:

You ask, by what interest did I get a ship? I answer, having served with credit was my recommendation to Lord Howe, First Lord of the Admiralty. Anything in reason that I can ask I am sure of obtaining from his justice.[12]

CREATING CONTROVERSY

Although peace now prevailed, the new appointment was to be a challenge. The *Boreas* sailed for the Leeward Islands, where the outcome of the recent war had created a new and difficult political situation. As Nelson put it:

The Americans, when colonists, possessed almost all the trade from America to our West India Islands;... on the return of peace they forgot on this occasion that they became foreigners and... had no right to trade in the British colonies.[13]

The Americans' new political independence now excluded them, under Britain's Navigation Laws, from continuing their former direct commerce with the British West Indies. Neither the Americans nor the West Indian colonists wished to comply with laws demanding that colonial products including cotton, sugar and tobacco be sent back to Britain before being re-shipped to a purchaser outside the empire; and that all goods entering British colonies had to be shipped from a port in Britain.

Considering his duty to stem from his commission as a British officer, Nelson tried to enforce the Navigation Laws. However, when he threatened to seize American vessels trading to the Islands, he found that the colonial governors, custom-house officers and other colonists both opposed and shunned him. When he actually attempted such a seizure, he was sued for assault with threats of imprisonment and damages. 'Persecuted from one island to another', he soon

Prince William Henry (1765-1837) as a midshipman, instructed by Admiral Digby. The Prince, third son of George III, became a competent sea officer, though lacking tact and judgement. Nelson maintained a regular correspondence with him after they ceased to serve together. The Prince acceded as William IV in 1830.

could not leave his ship. 'The residents of these islands are Americans by connexion and by interest and are inimical to Great Britain,' he fumed. 'They are as great rebels as ever were in America.'[14]

When the issue was eventually considered at the Admiralty Nelson claimed that he was supported from Britain, but the various incidents and the litigation they generated, which was still in progress when he returned to London in 1787, probably damaged his reputation. Together they created the impression of a man who was difficult to deal with on account of his ambition. In 1785 at Antigua, for example, Nelson refused to accept the authority of Commissioner Moutray to command him as a commodore on the grounds that he was a civilian, even though that authority had been granted by Admiral Hughes, the senior officer on the Leeward Islands station. In 1786, when he himself became senior officer, he rashly supported Prince William, who now had command of the *Pegasus*, against Lieutenant Isaac Schomberg, whom the Prince unwisely accused of neglect of duty. Schomberg requested a court martial on himself and Nelson went so far as to have him arrested, though Schomberg was shortly afterwards returned to England where the matter was quietly forgotten. Also in December 1786, Nelson wrongly supported the Prince against the Storekeeper at English Harbour, Antigua, who correctly required, but was refused, a completed muster book for the *Pegasus*. In his own defence, the Storekeeper had to send the copied correspondence to the Navy Board, which referred it to the Admiralty. It showed that Nelson had contradicted both written regulations and his own compliance with them; that he had put the Storekeeper in an improper and humiliating position and had acted more in his own than the public interest.

FRUSTRATIONS ASHORE

In all this Nelson clearly, and misguidedly, regarded his relationship with Prince William as of paramount importance. He had begun to court a widow, Frances Nisbet, during visits to the island of Nevis and, on the Prince insisting he should give the bride away, their marriage was arranged for 11 March 1787 when Nelson's royal subordinate was available. In June the *Boreas* sailed for home, to be diverted there to the impress service before being paid off in November. In England, with his new bride, Nelson went to live in the parsonage house at Burnham Thorpe. He tried unsuccessfully to obtain a place for his wife in the official household of Prince William Henry and visited Lord Hood, who became an Admiralty commissioner in July 1788, to enquire for new sea employment. But even in 1790, when relations with Spain came near to war over an incident at Nootka Sound, he could get nothing. Lord Hood saw him again but 'made a speech never to be effaced from my memory, viz. that the King was impressed with an unfavourable opinion of me'.[15] There was also, he later acknowledged, 'a prejudice at the Admiralty evidently against me'.[16] It was a difficult time, with only country life, Norfolk society and farming to distract him. Aggravating the situation was a writ for damages, assessed at £20,000, which a bailiff served on his wife one morning when he was out, for losses incurred by two American captains in his West Indian attempts to enforce the Navigation Laws. Fortunately the matter was later dropped. Meanwhile, since 1789, the French Revolution had been creating alarm and uncertainty throughout Europe. In Norfolk, Nelson had sympathy with the hardships of local agricultural labourers but not with the subversive corresponding societies spreading through the country. In early 1793 he had promises of a ship.

FANNY

Mrs Frances Nisbet was the daughter of a judge on the island of Nevis, whose first husband, a doctor, had died leaving her with a small son. She was keeping house for her wealthy uncle John Herbert, President of the Council on Nevis, when Nelson met her and they were married there on 11 March 1787. Returning to England in December, they spent five years at Burnham Thorpe before Nelson went back to sea in 1793 and their lives became steadily more separate. They had no children.

Frances Nelson (1761-1831): drawn in 1798 at the time her husband became involved with Lady Hamilton. By Daniel Orme (1767-c.1832).

Lace overskirt of Frances Nelson's wedding dress, 1787.

'Fanny' became devoted to Nelson's father, but her inefficiency and anxiety increasingly irritated her husband, who needed practical arrangements at home and craved expressions of support and admiration. As he fell under Lady Hamilton's spell, from late 1798, he refused Fanny's requests to join him in Italy and on return to England with the Hamiltons he continued to live with them. Nelson finally abandoned Fanny in March 1801, making provision for her but ruthlessly ignoring her attempts at reconciliation.

Ridiculed by Lady Hamilton and deserted by most of Nelson's family, Fanny's loyalty to Nelson remained constant. Her son Josiah rose to be a naval captain, largely through Nelson's influence. He was not a good officer but later had prosperous business interests in France, dying a year before his mother.

The execution of Louis XVI, on 21 January, and the formal outbreak of war with France on 1 February clinched the matter. A more friendly Lord Hood informed Nelson he had the 64-gun *Agamemnon*, fitting out at Chatham. He joined her in early February and by mid-April was back at sea where his undimmed ambition could be served.

THE REVOLUTIONARY WAR

In May 1793 the *Agamemnon* sailed as part of Lord Hood's fleet destined for the Mediterranean. There, with a French republican army closing on Marseilles and Toulon from the north,

Victory leaving the Channel in May 1793, outward bound with the fleet for Toulon and flying Lord Hood's flag as Vice-Admiral of the Red. By Monamy Swaine.

Toulon suddenly surrendered to Hood's force. It was an event to be wondered at: 'such an one as history cannot produce its equal; that the strongest place in Europe and twenty-two sail of the line etc., should be given up without firing a shot. It is not to be credited.'[17] Rather than share the developments at Toulon, Nelson was dispatched to request allied troops for its defence. His destination was Naples, joint-capital with Palermo of the Kingdom of the Two Sicilies which embraced Sicily and most of Italy south of Rome. There he met not only King Ferdinand but the British ambassador and his wife, Sir William and Emma, Lady Hamilton. With the

The good anchorage of San Fiorenzo Bay, north Corsica, was guarded by the ancient Mortella (myrtle) Point watchtower. Its tough resistance to British attack in 1794 made it the model for Britain's own Martello Towers built along the south coast from 1806. The tower was blown up when the British left but part still stands. The print (top) is from the Naval Chronicle, *1809; the photograph was taken in 1976.*

help of Sir John Acton, King Ferdinand's half-English prime minister, Nelson secured a promise of reinforcements and made some friends. After returning to Toulon and supporting a diplomatic mission to the governor of Tunis, he cruised off Corsica, where island nationalists were in revolt against French control. The siege of Toulon by French revolutionary forces was now drawing to a close. As the port's land defences were overrun by the republican army, the British succeeded in extracting a few French ships and burning some others but left most to form the nucleus of an enemy fleet. Driven from the harbour, the British then had to find a new base. Hood decided on Corsica, which commanded the trade route down the west coast of Italy and supplied naval stores to Toulon. An advance party of British troops landed to take the north-western port of San Fiorenzo. This would serve as the main British fleet base but its security also depended on the removal of French troops holding the fortress towns of Bastia and Calvi, especially as they were liable to form the focus of reinforcement from France.

CORSICA

Nelson urged Hood to capture Bastia, volunteering to direct the naval part of the attack. Even after he discovered that the French garrison was at least three times the available British force, he kept the information to himself, urging Hood to commit those troops he had: 'What would the immortal Wolfe have done? As he did, beat the Enemy, if he perished in the attempt.'[18] Hood responded by giving command of the landings and the construction of batteries to Nelson. After a five-week siege, the town surrendered in May 1794, principally because of hunger rather than the bombardment. Nelson was mortified when Hood's public report of the capture failed to give him the credit he felt was his due:

And when I reflect that I was the cause of re-attacking Bastia after our wise Generals gave it over from not knowing the force, fancying it over 2,000 men; that it was I, who, landing, joined the Corsicans, and only with my Ship's party of Marines drove the French under the walls of Bastia; that it was I, who, knowing the force in Bastia to be upwards of 4,000 men, as I have now only ventured to tell Lord Hood, landed with only 1,200 men, and kept the secret till within this week past; what I must have felt during the siege may be easily conceived. Yet I am scarcely mentioned....[19]

The siege of Bastia was quickly followed by that of Calvi. Here bombardment by land batteries also seemed the only means of reducing the town and Nelson was again made responsible for getting the guns in place. Landing them in a narrow, rocky inlet, then hauling them some two miles over rough, boulder-strewn terrain, much of it uphill, presented numerous challenges.

Nevertheless, after two weeks' work the batteries were under construction. Both this and the bombardment were dangerous as the British guns were within range of those on the walls of the town. Casualties were common; on 8 July three of the guns were damaged or destroyed and on 12 July Nelson himself was wounded. At first he thought little of it. A shot hit the sandbags of the rampart, driving sand and stones into his face. Apart from much blood and bruising there was little apparent injury. He did not mention to his wife the damage to his right eye until 4 August, only describing the consequences on the 18th:

I most fortunately escaped by only having my right eye nearly deprived of its sight. It was cut down, but as far recovered as to be able to distinguish light from darkness, but as to all the purpose of its use it is gone. However, the blemish is nothing, not to be perceived unless told.[20]

The pupil developed a slightly enlarged, fixed look and he never regained useful sight in that eye.

A NEW OBJECTIVE

Nelson otherwise survived the siege in good health, although half the men involved sickened from malaria, dysentery or typhoid. On 10 August, short of ammunition, the French surrendered and Nelson again felt he was not given the credit he deserved in Lord Hood's official report, published in the *London Gazette*:

Others, for keeping succours out of Calvi for a few summer months are handsomely mentioned. Such things are... my heart... is full when I think of the treatment I have received: every man who had any considerable share in the reduction has got some place or other – I, only I, am without reward. Nothing but my anxious endeavours to serve my country makes me bear up against it; but I sometimes am ready to give all up.[21]

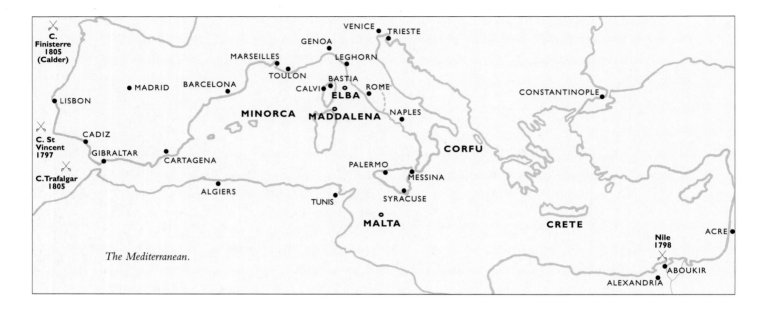

The Mediterranean.

His spirits revived once he was at sea again. That autumn, to help harry the French army pushing south into Italy, he went to negotiate British use of the harbour at Genoa. He was also sent to look into Toulon where there were 22 ships in the outer harbour. The activity suited him. By the end of October 1794, he did not think he had ever been so truly well; the climate had done him good and he had 'grown quite stout'. He also had confidence in his crew who were taking time to recover from the sickness brought on by shore operations. In October he still had 77 on the sick list, 'almost all objects for the Hospital'[22], and he had also lost men to other ships; yet he was sure the remainder felt themselves 'equal to go alongside any seventy-four out of France'.[23] Their recovery was aided at

the end of the year by the need to refit the *Agamemnon* at Leghorn. Nelson, however, was miserable lying in port and preferred the storms and gales of wind experienced in blockading Toulon that winter.

Lord Hood, who was now 'very well inclined' towards Nelson, went home in mid-October, relinquishing command to Vice-Admiral Sir William Hotham. Nelson enjoyed less credit with Hotham, who also had less influence at the Admiralty than Hood. It was thus clear that, if he wanted recognition and promotion, he would have to distinguish himself in action to such a degree that his part could not be overlooked in Hotham's reports. From the winter of 1794–5, Nelson's philosophy and course to achieve his ambitions were fixed.

Bromley del.

Worthington sculp.

LOSS OF HIS EYE BEFORE CALVI.

*Site of Nelson's battery,
photographed in 1955
by Cmdr. J.A. Quarrie.
The white patch on the rock
is a modern French plaque
(then itself well bullet-holed)
commemorating Nelson's
injury there.*

*An 1808 print of the
incident in which Nelson
lost the sight of his right eye
when a shot hit the parapet
of his battery on 12 July
1794, during the capture
of Corsica.*

THE DECADE OF VICTORIES, 1795–1805

BY 1795, Nelson was thirty-six years old, a captain of nearly fifteen years seniority, and in command of the 64-gun, Fourth-Rate ship of the line, *Agamemnon*. His experience was wide in terms of seamanship, exploration, general naval service, minor skirmishes and amphibious operations, but he had never done what most regarded as the primary role of a naval officer – engaged a fleet of enemy ships in combat – or, for that matter, fought a major single-ship action.

Wax profile of Nelson, 1805: by Catherine Andras (1775-1860) whose other sitters included the family of George III.

In March 1795 the *Agamemnon* was still in the Mediterranean Fleet under Vice-Admiral Hotham, an ineffective, stop-gap officer. For once, the French fleet was active in the area, and on 12 March they were sighted off Corsica. Hotham had 14 ships of the line; the French had 15, but they were larger and very heavily manned because they were carrying troops as well as sailors. A chase began, though the French were some miles ahead, their ships were cleaner and they could sail better. Captain Fremantle in the frigate *Inconstant* noticed that the 80-gun *Ça Ira** was disabled, and got into a position to rake her. Nelson came to support him in the *Agamemnon*; he chased the *Ça Ira*, turning occasionally to fire his broadside, to such effect that the French ship suffered over 100 casualties. Nelson had only seven men wounded but found himself too far in advance of his own fleet and was forced to give up the chase.

Hotham was an admiral of the old, over-cautious school. On the evening of 12 March he wasted time by forming his fleet into textbook

* *'That will happen': the title of a French Revolutionary song.*

order of sailing, rather than ordering a general chase. Two days later he sighted the enemy fleet again, with the *Ça Ira* being towed by the 74-gun *Censeur*. Despite the efforts of the French to protect them, both were captured by several ships including the *Agamemnon*. Hotham was satisfied at that and let the rest of the French go. Nelson was not; he went on board the flagship, in a state of some agitation, and urged Hotham to pursue. The Admiral, in a much cooler frame of mind, ignored the insubordination and commented, 'We must be contented. We have done very well.' Nelson wrote to his wife in characteristic terms: 'had we taken ten sail, and allowed the 11th to escape when it had been possible to have got at

The capture of the Ça Ira, *80 guns, in Hotham's action, 13-14 March 1795. The* Ça Ira *lost two masts in collision, and while under tow was attacked by the frigate* Inconstant, *Captain Fremantle. Nelson then single-handedly attacked in the 64-gun* Agamemnon *for two hours, and again, with others, the following day until the* Ça Ira *and the ship towing her, the* Censeur, *surrendered. By Nicholas Pocock.*

her, I could never call it well done.'[1] Hotham took into account the shot damage to his fleet's rigging, the fact that repair facilities and stores were almost non-existent and the isolation of the British in the Mediterranean. Nelson was more conscious of the deterioration of discipline and morale among the French as a consequence of the Revolution. His subsequent career tends to prove him right but for the moment Hotham was triumphant; he was voted the thanks of both Houses of Parliament and was promoted to full admiral.

The battle was insignificant but it gives early evidence of Nelson's attitudes to combat. He showed his keen tactical awareness: in the right place at the right time to harass the *Ça Ira*, he immediately did so, handling his ship with great skill. In arguing with his admiral, he demonstrated his belief that subordination and hierarchy were means, not ends in themselves. And in his desperation to pursue the enemy, he showed his insatiable desire for victory.

NAVAL TACTICS

The modern age in naval tactics had begun during the first Anglo-Dutch war of 1651–4, when the English navy discovered the 'line of battle'. Since ships carried most of their guns on the broadside, they were most effective if the fleet formed a single line, with one ship behind another so that no ship's guns were masked. The great disadvantage of the line was that it was mainly defensive: it could fire only sideways and could not advance on an enemy and fire at the same time. Over the next century, the Royal Navy became increasingly dominated by regulations, and admirals were virtually obliged to form line of battle before an engagement. After the Battle of Toulon in 1744, the technical basis for Admiral Mathews being dismissed the service was that he did not form a proper line before engaging.

A new epoch began in 1747 when, in two successive battles off Cape Finisterre, Admirals Anson and Hawke both found enemy convoys protected by men of war. Both ordered a general chase, confident of their great numerical superiority, and captured several enemy ships. Old attitudes persisted, however. Off Minorca in 1756 Admiral Byng remembered the Toulon fiasco and was too cautious in his approach. For this and other sins, he was made a political scapegoat, court-martialled and shot. At Quiberon Bay in November 1759 Admiral Hawke went to the opposite extreme. In a rising gale and a battle worthy of Nelson himself, he chased the French fleet into the bay and virtually annihilated it as a fighting force.

In this way, a new school of tacticians began to emerge, committed to the enemy's destruction rather than preservation of the line of battle. There were two main ways to attack an enemy decisively. One was to break his line, either by single ships or in squadrons, and reduce it to chaos. When passing through the line, each of the attacking ships was also in a position to fire its full broadsides into the weak bows and sterns of the opposing vessels, 'raking' their internal decks from end to end. The other method was to 'double' the enemy: force was concentrated on part of his line, preferably with one ship on either side of individual enemy vessels. Breaking the line and doubling were both risky, in that the attackers' initial approach made them vulnerable to a determined enemy; but this was offset by the fact that the British navy's fighting skill increased over the next few decades, while its opponents' tended to decline. Thus the chances of decisive action became ever more likely.

The old and new schools of tactics co-existed throughout the American War of 1776–83. The Battle of Ushant in 1778 was an old-fashioned, indecisive line action. At the West Indian Battle of the Saints four years later, Admiral Sir George Rodney broke the French line, perhaps a little reluctantly and partly owing to a shift of wind. The result was none the less a decisive victory, with the capture of the French flagship.

The first great fleet battle of the French Revolutionary War was fought well out in the Atlantic on the 'Glorious First of June' 1794 (see page 52). The British commander, Lord Howe, was a competent but notoriously cautious admiral. The main French objective was to find and protect a large grain convoy, with the result that French evasive manoeuvres allowed the British

NAVAL TACTICS

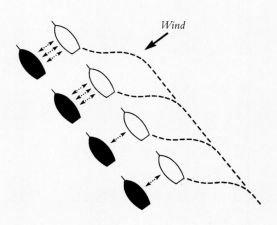

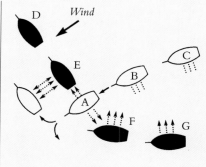

(2) BREAKING THE LINE

White breaks Black's line and engages to leeward. A rakes E from astern and F from ahead in passing. B and C unable to return broadsides of F and G during the approach. D may not be able to turn and help E, F and G until too late.

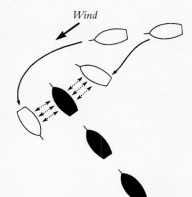

(1) LINE ACTION

White, to windward, has the advantage of the 'weather gauge'; Black engaging to leeward (lee gauge).

(3) DOUBLING

White doubles the head of Black's line and engages the lead ship(s) at odds of two to one; in principle, Nelson's tactic at the Nile.

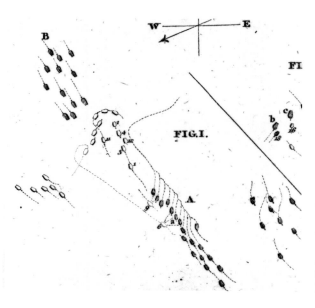

Nelson in the Captain wears out of British line to block the Spanish retreat at Cape St Vincent, supported by Collingwood's Excellent (not shown) and Troubridge in the Culloden. From Steel's Naval Chronologist, 1802.

Bell of the San Josef,
dated 1792.

The Battle of Cape St Vincent, 14 February 1797. *'Nelson's patent bridge for boarding First Rates' shown in a painting by Sir William Allen (1782-1850). Nelson in the* Captain *(left) boards and takes the Spanish* San Nicolas *as the latter runs foul of the three-decker* San Josef*, 114 guns. He goes on to take this too.*

three days to get their fleet into position for the main attack. Having finally brought the enemy to battle, Howe gave orders to break their line; only 5 of his ships succeeded in doing so but, in the mêlée that ensued, 6 out of 26 French ships were captured and one was sunk. However, because the convoy escaped, both sides claimed victory.

NELSON AT ST VINCENT

Nelson chafed under Hotham's command for some months, blockading enemy ports and attacking their supply routes. Sir John Jervis, who took over the Mediterranean fleet in December 1795, was much more to his taste. Though Jervis was no great risk-taker, he was a dynamic commander and urged his captains on to greater activity. He was also a fierce disciplinarian with strong opinions, who restricted officers' privileges if they conflicted with the demands of duty and was not afraid to condemn captains or even admirals if he thought them inadequate. He had already noticed Nelson, his zeal and his lack

Nelson boarding the San Josef *at Cape St Vincent, by George Jones (1786-1869).*

of discretion and used influence to have him promoted to commodore so that he was eligible to command a small squadron.

As French armies overran large parts of Italy, Britain found itself short of reliable allies or strong bases in the area and, late in 1796, the government decided to withdraw from the Mediterranean. Nelson organized the evacuation of Corsica and Jervis, based at Gibraltar, concentrated on blockading the Spanish fleet in its Atlantic ports, especially Cadiz. On 14 February 1797 the Spanish fleet attempted to sail from Cartagena to Cadiz and was met by the British

off Cape St Vincent. That day, Nelson first showed the world his great abilities. The Spaniards, comprising 27 ships of the line, were sailing through the night in their anxiety to reach Cadiz and were split into two groups, in no particular formation. Jervis had 15 of the line rigidly deployed in two columns, which he began to form into a single line of battle before tacking in succession towards the largest body of the enemy. It was a slow procedure and might have allowed the bulk of the Spanish fleet to escape. Nelson, now in the 74-gun *Captain* towards the rear of the British line, was the first to see a more

Nelson wounded at Tenerife, 24 July 1797. *While landing he was hit just above the right elbow by a musket ball, shattering the bone and joint. The arm was amputated aboard the* Theseus *that night. Nelson's stepson, Lieutenant Josiah Nisbet, stands behind him in this picture by Richard Westall, one of the set illustrating the 1809* Life of Nelson.

direct means of attack. He took his ship out of the line, wore round, and aimed to head-off the van of the main enemy force. In doing so he technically broke his orders, a situation which would have been unthinkable to a previous generation. Jervis, however, spotted the same opportunity soon afterwards and signalled others to the same effect.

Nelson was supported by Captain Cuthbert Collingwood in the *Excellent*, who also fell out of line to follow him. Meanwhile the *Culloden*, at the head of the British line, left off the attack on the enemy rear and headed straight for the van, supported by several other ships. A pell-mell battle broke out round the head of the Spanish line. Nelson watched two Spanish ships, the *San Nicolas* of 80 guns and the *San Josef* of 114, colliding in the confusion. The *Captain* was already damaged but he took her alongside the *San Nicolas*. He then personally led the boarding party

Sir Thomas Fremantle, Vice-Admiral of the Blue (1765-1819), distinguished himself in frigates and was severely wounded with Nelson at Tenerife, 1797, in command of the Seahorse. *He commanded the* Ganges *at the Battle of Copenhagen and the* Neptune *at Trafalgar, where the Spanish flagship* Santissima Trinidad *surrendered to him. The diary of his wife, Betsey Wynne (who was with him at Tenerife), says much about him and Nelson's other captains. After a portrait by Domenico Pellegrini.*

which captured the *San Nicolas* and, from her, the *San Josef*, one after the other. The fleet quickly dubbed the feat 'Nelson's patent bridge for boarding First Rates'.[2] Two other Spanish ships were captured but the victory is also notable for the way in which the British triumphed against numerical odds of nearly two to one.

Sir John Jervis was amply rewarded. He was created Earl of St Vincent, a higher rank in the peerage than Nelson was ever to attain. Nelson, who had contributed more to the victory than anyone else, was knighted and became a national hero for the first time.

Two weeks before the battle, though he only heard later, the Admiralty had promoted Nelson to Rear-Admiral of the Blue. In July 1797 he led a squadron of four 74-gun ships, a 50, three frigates and two smaller vessels to try to capture two Spanish treasure ships sheltering with others in the well-defended harbour of Santa Cruz in Tenerife. About 1,100 seamen and marines were landed and succeeded in capturing the town, where they found themselves surrounded by a force of about 8,000 Spaniards. A truce was agreed and the British were allowed to withdraw to their ships, with 141 men killed and 105 wounded, Nelson among them. While landing, his right elbow had been shattered by a musket ball and he had been immediately taken back to the *Theseus*, whose surgeon amputated his arm that night.

While Nelson was recovering from his wound in England a decisive battle took place off Camperdown, on the Dutch coast. Admiral Adam Duncan, with a squadron of 16 ships of the line, engaged a Dutch force of equal numbers but smaller ships. He approached the enemy line at right angles, risking the full effect of their guns before he could bring his own to bear. Fully aware that Dutch ships had shallower draughts than British, he also risked grounding by breaking the Dutch line and going inshore of it, in their home waters. He captured 11 Dutch ships in a victory which showed similar qualities to Nelson's in daring and tactical skill. But the Dutch did not pose the same threat as their French allies and Duncan was no great self-publicist; Camperdown attracted much less notice from the general public, and from later historians, than Nelson's battles.

THE NILE CAMPAIGN

By the spring of 1798 Nelson was again fit for service and on 29 March he hoisted his flag aboard the *Vanguard*, a 74, with orders to rejoin the Earl of St Vincent off Cadiz. On 10 April he sailed from the Solent, with a convoy under escort. The Mediterranean was still empty of British warships but the French, inspired by Napoleon Bonaparte, had found a way to exploit their control of that sea and to attack British interests. Realizing that an invasion of Britain was impracticable, General Bonaparte suggested a daring scheme. Collecting troops, warships and transport vessels from Southern France and Northern Italy, he would land in Egypt, overthrow its Mameluke rulers and be in a strong position to attack British power in India.

By the time Nelson sailed, disturbing reports were reaching the Admiralty that the French were preparing large numbers of ships in Toulon, Genoa and elsewhere, though their purpose was unknown. They might launch an assault on Naples and the Two Sicilies or break out of the Mediterranean and attack Portugal or Ireland. No one had yet guessed their real destination, but the Admiralty was concerned enough to order St Vincent to 'act upon a plan of operations very different from what we have hitherto adopted...[and] attended with a considerable degree of

Captain Sir Thomas
Boulden Thompson
(1766-1828). At the Battle
of the Nile, Thompson
commanded the Leander,
50 guns, which was later
captured by the Généreux,
one of two French ships of
the line which escaped, while
taking home dispatches. He
was knighted on his release
for the stout defence he had
made. In 1801 he lost a leg
as captain of the Bellona,
74 guns, at Copenhagen.
He died and was buried at
Greenwich as Comptroller of
Greenwich Hospital. After a
miniature by J.D. Engleheart.

LEFT Sir Edward Berry,
Rear-Admiral of the Blue
(1768.-1831). Berry,
like Nelson, came from
Norfolk. He was Nelson's
first lieutenant in the
Agamemnon and, as a
commander and volunteer
in the Captain, fought with
him at Cape St Vincent.
He then became his flag-
captain in the Vanguard
during the Nile campaign
and, in Thompson's
Leander, was captured
taking home the dis-
patches. At Trafalgar
Berry commanded the
Agamemnon. By
John Singleton Copley
(1737-1815).

Sir Alexander Ball, Rear-
Admiral of the Red (1757-
1809). Ball's Alexander,
74 guns, saved Nelson's
Vanguard by taking her in
tow when dismasted by storm
in 1798, and also fought at
the Nile. He then blockaded
the French on Malta and,
when the island fell in 1800,

became its first governor. Of
Nelson he wrote that
'though his temper was …
irritable and uneven, yet
never was a commander so
enthusiastically loved by men
of all ranks from the captain
of the fleet to the youngest
ship-boy.' By Henry
Pickersgill (1782-1875).

risk'. A squadron was to be sent into the
Mediterranean, despite the great weakness of the
British position there.

Nelson rejoined St Vincent on 30 April. The
First Lord of the Admiralty had already hinted to
St Vincent that he should be given a special role:
*If you determine to send a detachment into the
Mediterranean, I think it almost unnecessary to suggest
to you the propriety of putting it under the command of
Sir H. Nelson, whose acquaintance with that part of
the World, as well as his activity and disposition, seem
to qualify him in a peculiar manner for that service.*[3]

St Vincent needed most of his ships to blockade the Spanish in Cadiz but he decided to send
Nelson on an armed reconnaissance. He was
given a force of three 74-gun ships: his flagship
Vanguard, the *Alexander* and the *Orion*, with five
frigates. His orders were to 'endeavour to ascer-
tain, by every means in your power, either upon
the coasts of Provence or Genoa, the object of
the [French] equipment, the destination of which

Sir Thomas Foley, Admiral of the White (1757-1833). Foley was second flag-captain at Toulon in 1793 and at Cape St Vincent. He led Nelson's fleet into action at the Nile in the Goliath, 74 guns, being able to make the final commitment to outflank the French by having the most up-to-date local charts – ironically, French ones. At Copenhagen in 1801 he was Nelson's temporary flag-captain in the Elephant, 74 guns. Nelson later asked him to be captain of the fleet, but he declined on health grounds and missed Trafalgar. He died as commander-in-chief at Portsmouth, this miniature showing him in later life with his St Vincent and Nile medals. Attributed to William Grimaldi (1751-1830).

is differently spoken of.'[4] By 20 May he was off the southern French coast, 'being exactly in a situation for intercepting the enemy ships bound into Marseilles, Toulon &c'.[5] Unknown to Nelson, the main body of Napoleon's force had already sailed on the 19th.

Nelson's squadron was then hit by bad luck, or as he put it to his wife: 'I firmly believe, that it was the Almighty's goodness, to check my consummate vanity.'[6] Towards midnight on the 20th, a strong gale blew up without warning and within two hours the *Vanguard* was almost completely dismasted. She drifted for nearly two days until the storm abated and she was taken in tow by the *Alexander* under Captain Ball. The three 74s reached the southern end of Sardinia on the 24th, having lost contact with the frigates during the storm. A lesser man might have abandoned the mission and returned to Gibraltar for repairs but Nelson anchored off the island of San Pietro and began to fit the *Vanguard* with jury masts.

Unfortunately, Captain Hope, senior officer of the frigates, failed to predict his movements. Having searched for Nelson for some time, he eventually returned to Gibraltar, leaving Nelson's reconnaissance force without its most essential element – frigates.

Nelson returned to a position off Toulon, arriving on 5 June. There he met the naval brig *Mutine*, with better news: reinforcements were on the way. Two days later he was joined by 10 more 74-gun ships, plus the 50-gun *Leander*. St Vincent had decided to upgrade his squadron into a real fighting unit. He had detached many of his best ships and replaced them with others from England; but he was unaware of Nelson's lack of frigates and this deficiency was to have serious effects.

Now knowing that Bonaparte had sailed, Nelson immediately searched for him down the coast of Italy. He anchored off Naples and, from Sir William Hamilton, learnt that the French had gone to attack Malta. After he passed through the Straits of Messina a merchant ship told him that Bonaparte had captured, garrisoned and then left Malta. Since the wind was a steady westerly, Nelson correctly deduced that the enemy must have gone east and that the most likely destination was Egypt. With his customary zeal he set course for Alexandria. This was unfortunate, as Bonaparte was cautious at sea and had a large, slow fleet of transports to protect. Instead of taking a direct route, he had sailed via the coast of Crete. The two fleets passed closely on 22 June when, indeed, some of the outlying units of the French were sighted. Nelson had no frigates, however; he had to keep his ships of the line together and had no other vessel he could send to investigate. On the 28th he arrived off Alexandria and was distressed to find no sign of the French. He sailed back to Syracuse in Sicily, where he at last had a chance for proper repairs to be made to the *Vanguard* and for his ships to take on stores.

Nelson's decision to leave Alexandria had again been unfortunate, for the French arrived two days later. The army disembarked and on 21 July defeated the Mamelukes at the Battle of the Pyramids. The French naval force – 13 of the line and four frigates under Admiral Brueys – anchored in line across Aboukir Bay, in a position which was considered strong against fleet attack.

Nelson's squadron left Syracuse on 23 July. He went to Crete to look for the French and there learnt that they had indeed gone to Egypt. He immediately sailed for Alexandria and arrived off

The Battle of the Nile, 1 August 1798. *The start of the action, looking north-west across Aboukir Bay at sunset. Nelson's fleet, led by Captain Foley's* Goliath, *is in the process of doubling the head of the anchored French line, with the Aboukir fort beyond. By Nicholas Pocock.*

the port at noon on 1 August. Disappointingly, no ships of the line could be seen, but the squadron proceeded eastwards and at 2.30pm the *Theseus* signalled that an enemy fleet was in sight, at anchor. Although it would no longer be possible to fight the action in daylight, Nelson decided to attack right away.

The French were unprepared. Although they had four frigates, none had been sent out to look for Nelson. Their ships were anchored by the bow only and would swing according to the wind and current. Their guns were only ready on the seaward side and hundreds of men were ashore on watering parties or as armed escorts.

LEFT *The destruction of* L'Orient *at the Battle of the Nile. The flagship of Admiral François Brueys exploding at about 10pm, with a blast heard 15 miles away in Alexandria. It so shocked both sides that firing ceased for several minutes. The ship in the centre is the* Swiftsure, *commanded by the Canadian, Benjamin Hallowell, who remained engaged until the explosion. By George Arnald (1763-1841).*

BELOW LEFT *Lightning conductor from* L'Orient's *mainmast. Nelson kept this in the hall of his house at Merton as a souvenir. His coffin, also made from the mast, was a gift from Captain Hallowell.*

The French had neither time nor resources to rectify the situation. As he led the advance on the French line, Captain Foley of the *Goliath* noticed an even greater flaw in its position. It was clear that the leading French ship was far enough from the shore to allow another vessel to pass ahead of it and attack from the landward side. It has never been established exactly how much Foley acted on his own initiative in doing this and how much had been agreed in advance with Nelson. In any case, it was characteristic of Nelson's style that a captain was allowed such initiative.

The other ships arrived one by one, action beginning at about 6.30pm. The first few followed Foley; others stayed on the seaward side to achieve a classic doubling manoeuvre on the French, while a few broke through the line to increase the devastation. In the middle of the battle,

now in darkness, the French flagship *L'Orient* blew up, with great loss of life. Having captured or destroyed the ships at the head of the French line, Nelson moved against those further down, which had so far been largely passive. Out of a total of 13 French ships of the line and 4 frigates, only 2 of the line and 2 frigates escaped, making it one of the most decisive actions in naval history. Although the victory is indelibly stamped with Nelson's name, he left all the initiative to his captains and made no signals for 11 hours, during the heat of the battle. He had in fact sustained a bad scalp wound on his forehead and was taken below, believing his life or his sight to be in danger.

The Nile campaign had been an epic of naval warfare. For three months Nelson had led a squadron with virtually no reference to higher

Haberdashers quickly produced ribbons with Nelsonic designs to celebrate the Battle of the Nile; this is an example.

This musket and canteen were among the gifts which the Sultan of Turkey, Selim III, showered on Nelson after the Battle of the Nile. The silver Nile Cup, by Paul Storr of London, 1799, was given by London's 'Turkey merchants', the chartered 'Company of Merchants trading in the Levant Seas'.

Bilston enamel patch boxes (for cosmetic use) and a gold anchor necklace, all celebrating the Battle of the Nile; the anchor and chain is inscribed 'Admiral Nelson and the British Tars relieves the World at the mouth of the Nile 1st of August 1798'. The boxes were made in enormous numbers to commemorate Nelson's victories and death.

authority, making all his decisions on the basis of scanty evidence. He had been through extraordinary emotional highs and lows. He had recovered from a storm, failed and then succeeded in finding the French fleet and inflicted a uniquely crushing defeat on it. Turkey and Naples bestowed gifts and decorations on him and in Britain he became, for the first time as a fleet commander, the hero of the hour. He received a pension and a peerage, though as a baron rather than an earl, because he was not a commander-in-chief. Other consequences were less good. His head wound left severe concussive effects and prolonged stress now began to affect his health and state of mind; for it was in the following months that the most controversial events of his life occurred – the start of his affair with Lady Hamilton and his involvement in the execution of the Neapolitan jacobins. His infatuation with Emma was to bring scandal and ridicule; both developments raised further doubts as to his judgement outside strictly naval matters.

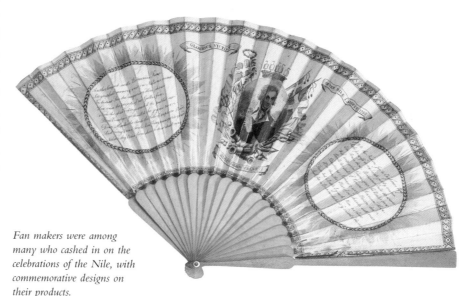

Fan makers were among many who cashed in on the celebrations of the Nile, with commemorative designs on their products.

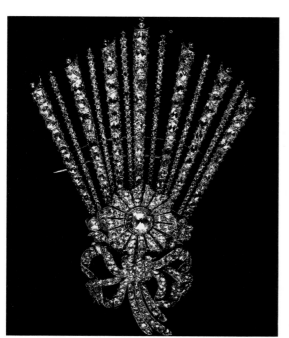

The chelengk: *the highest Turkish award for valour, given to Nelson by the Sultan after the Nile. It was a spray of Brazilian diamonds worn in the turban - or hat in Nelson's case - with a rotating central boss driven by clockwork. Stolen from Greenwich in 1951, it was probably broken up.*

CRISIS IN NAPLES

Late in 1798 the French invaded Neapolitan territory and that December Nelson evacuated their royal family to Palermo. Emma lent enthusiastic aid and the commander of the Neapolitan navy, Commodore Prince Caracciolo helped with the arrangements. In January 1799 French troops took Naples and, supported by local jacobins, set up the short-lived Parthenopean Republic. By June, however, King Ferdinand's war minister, Cardinal Ruffo, aided by Nelson's ships, had isolated the French garrison and negotiated a local truce. This provided for their departure and that of all Neapolitan rebels who wished to leave; thousands did, anticipating little mercy from Ferdinand. When Nelson arrived at Naples on 24 June he repudiated the truce as unauthorized by the King, a decision that Ferdinand quickly confirmed. Nelson then stood by with merciless equanimity, and Lady Hamilton with unpleasant approval, as the Neapolitan royalists exacted 'justice' on supposed republicans of all social ranks, men and women alike; hundreds were executed

FIGHTING WEAPONS

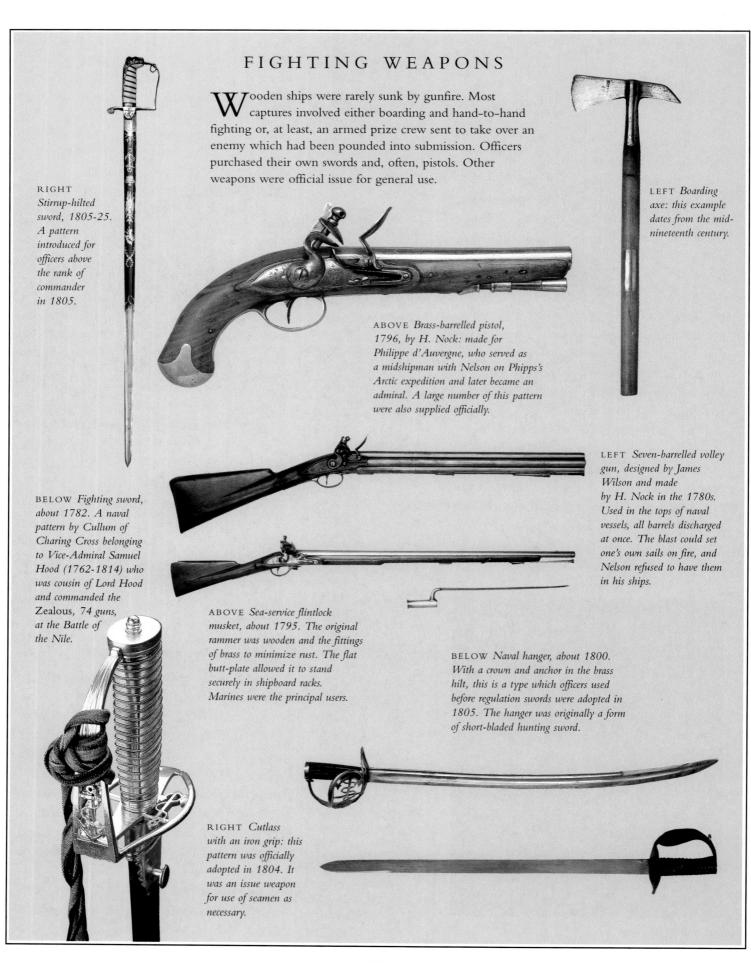

Wooden ships were rarely sunk by gunfire. Most captures involved either boarding and hand-to-hand fighting or, at least, an armed prize crew sent to take over an enemy which had been pounded into submission. Officers purchased their own swords and, often, pistols. Other weapons were official issue for general use.

RIGHT *Stirrup-hilted sword, 1805-25. A pattern introduced for officers above the rank of commander in 1805.*

LEFT *Boarding axe: this example dates from the mid-nineteenth century.*

ABOVE *Brass-barrelled pistol, 1796, by H. Nock: made for Philippe d'Auvergne, who served as a midshipman with Nelson on Phipps's Arctic expedition and later became an admiral. A large number of this pattern were also supplied officially.*

BELOW *Fighting sword, about 1782. A naval pattern by Cullum of Charing Cross belonging to Vice-Admiral Samuel Hood (1762-1814) who was cousin of Lord Hood and commanded the Zealous, 74 guns, at the Battle of the Nile.*

LEFT *Seven-barrelled volley gun, designed by James Wilson and made by H. Nock in the 1780s. Used in the tops of naval vessels, all barrels discharged at once. The blast could set one's own sails on fire, and Nelson refused to have them in his ships.*

ABOVE *Sea-service flintlock musket, about 1795. The original rammer was wooden and the fittings of brass to minimize rust. The flat butt-plate allowed it to stand securely in shipboard racks. Marines were the principal users.*

BELOW *Naval hanger, about 1800. With a crown and anchor in the brass hilt, this is a type which officers used before regulation swords were adopted in 1805. The hanger was originally a form of short-bladed hunting sword.*

RIGHT *Cutlass with an iron grip: this pattern was officially adopted in 1804. It was an issue weapon for use of seamen as necessary.*

PRESENTATION SWORDS

Dress swords were presented to officers as a mark of distinction. In particular, Lloyd's, the London insurance exchange, established a Patriotic Fund which from 1803 to 1810 awarded officers commemorative swords of 30, 50 or 100 guineas value, a variant on the last being the swords given to the captains who fought at Trafalgar in 1805. The Fund also gave presentations of plate and money. All the Patriotic Fund swords were made by Richard Teed and came with a special belt and sword knot in a mahogany case.

ABOVE *Presentation smallswords including Jervis's and Cockburn's (see below) second and fourth from the left.*

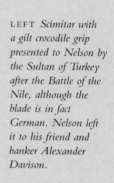

LEFT *Scimitar with a gilt crocodile grip presented to Nelson by the Sultan of Turkey after the Battle of the Nile, although the blade is in fact German. Nelson left it to his friend and banker Alexander Davison.*

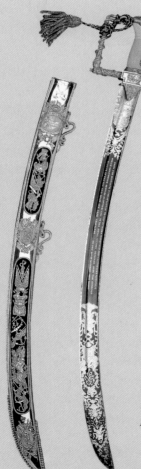

LEFT *Lloyd's Patriotic Fund Trafalgar sword of Captain Mansfield. He commanded the* Minotaur *at Trafalgar, capturing the Spanish* Neptune.

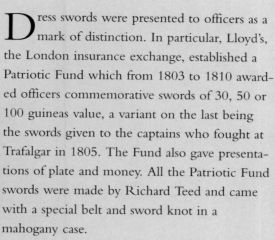

RIGHT *Detail of the gold and enamel hilt of the smallsword presented to Sir John Jervis by the City of London after the Battle of Cape St Vincent. By James Morisset and Robert Makepeace.*

ABOVE *Silver-gilt hilted smallsword given by Nelson to Captain George Cockburn of* La Minerve *in 1797 to commemorate their capture of the Spanish Santa Sabina, 19-20 December 1796.*

LEFT *Ferdinand IV, King of Naples and Sicily (1751-1825). 'Il re nasone' - 'King Nose': a valuable British ally but a dissolute and despotic ruler, he was twice driven temporarily from his throne. From 1816 he formally reigned as Ferdinand I of the Kingdom of the Two Sicilies. By Biaggio di Costanza.*

in scenes of savage carnival. Nelson ordered that the Neapolitan navy should court-martial Caracciolo, who had joined the rebels, and that on being found guilty he should be hanged at a Neapolitan yardarm and his body thrown into the sea. The bloated corpse rose some days later close to Nelson's flagship *Foudroyant*, deservedly shocking King Ferdinand who was then on board.

Given Nelson's hatred of French republicanism, his conviction of the need to uphold a British ally in the central Mediterranean and his own dictum 'that rewards and punishments are the foundation of all good government', his actions were understandable.[7] His own commitment to the corrupt Neapolitan monarchy was, however, a further instance of personal involvements overcoming professional detachment. It was an ugly episode and a reminder that where Nelson thought 'Some well-timed and speedy

RIGHT *Maria-Carolina, Queen of Naples (1752-1814). Austrian sister of the executed Marie-Antoinette. She was talkative, pious, astute and practically ran Naples for her husband. She also bore him eighteen children, over half of whom died. In Lady Hamilton she found a friend, confidante and a valued backstairs link with the British. Artist unknown.*

punishments will have the happiest effects' he could be as ferocious as the severe standards of his day allowed.[8] A grateful King Ferdinand made him Duke of Brontë, in Sicily. The Admiralty and Lord Keith, now Mediterranean commander-in-chief, took a much more censorious view of his personal attachments to Naples.

Nelson continued in the Mediterranean until 1800, for some time as acting commander-in-chief. His last action there was on 18 April that year. While sailing to the blockade of Malta with Keith, the squadron encountered the *Généreux*, one of the two French ships of the line which had escaped from the Nile. She surrendered after a short action with Nelson's *Foudroyant*, Keith's *Northumberland* and a frigate. The second Nile fugitive, the *Guillaume Tell*, was captured six weeks later.

Rear-Admiral Nelson, painted at Naples in 1798-99, by Leonardo Guzzardi. Better than any other portrait, this shows his exhausted appearance after the Nile campaign and how he wore his hat to keep it clear of the scar of his forehead wound. He wears his St Vincent medal and the chelengk. The scarlet pelisse or cloak which the Sultan gave him is over the chair.

BELOW *The fleet under Rear-Admiral Nelson at anchor in the Bay of Naples, 17 June 1798. An unusual view taken when Nelson called at Naples while searching for the French before the Battle of the Nile. Gouache drawing by Giacomo Guardi.*

COPENHAGEN

Nelson struck his flag in July 1800 and travelled home overland with Sir William and Lady Hamilton. He arrived in England in November but it was not until January 1801 that he was appointed to a new post, as second-in-command of the Channel Fleet under St Vincent, his flagship being the *San Josef*, which he had captured at the Battle of St Vincent. He was soon ordered to Great Yarmouth, however, for new service under Admiral Sir Hyde Parker.

Though the Mediterranean was now relatively secure, the concern of the government had turned to the Baltic, a vital source of timber, tar, hemp and other naval stores. The powers of the region – Russia, Denmark, Prussia and Sweden – had formed a northern confederation and declared their 'Armed Neutrality' in the conflict between Britain and France. In practice the alliance was weighted against Britain, as it denied the British claim to 'right of search' over neutral merchant ships, which was essential to the blockade of France. Parker's fleet was ordered to the Baltic and at the end of March he passed through

the Sound. Since the northern powers had not had time to combine their fleets, the first task was to tackle that of the Danes.

Like the French at the Nile, the Danes decided to fight at anchor, drawn up in front of their capital city, Copenhagen. In many ways their position was much stronger than Aboukir Bay. They were in home waters and could take advantage of the shoals of the area. Unlike the French, they had full warning of the enemy approach. They were close to their own shore batteries, normally almost invulnerable to attack by warships. There were no mistakes in anchoring, or in

Lady Hamilton (c.1761-1815) as 'Ariadne', by George Romney (1734-1802). Probably the best known of Romney's many studies of the young Emma: painted in 1785, the year after Sir William met her and was, like everyone else, captivated by her beauty.

leaving a navigable gap between the ships and the shore, or in having large numbers of men absent.

The main Danish line consisted of 7 unrigged ships of the line and 11 smaller vessels, fitted as floating batteries. These were anchored bow and stern to the south and east of the Trekroner battery, which was the keystone of the defence. Other ships blocked the harbour entrance to the west, and in front of the Danish line was the Middle Ground shoal. This prevented a direct approach by the British. The Danes had chosen to draw their ships up in line on the west side of the King's Deep channel, instead of using them to block its north and south entrances. Moreover, out of necessity they had deployed some very weak vessels as floating batteries, including some of less than 20 guns. The British approach was thus difficult but not impossible for an admiral of Nelson's calibre.

Nelson was given a squadron of 11 two-deckers and 6 frigates, specially chosen for their

shallow draught, while Parker remained in reserve north of the city with 8 larger ships of the line. Nelson sailed south by an offshore channel and anchored at the south end of the Middle Ground shoal on 1 April. He then waited for a southerly wind to carry him up the King's Deep alongside the Danish line. British knowledge of the area was sketchy. There were several pilots aboard but they were experienced in merchant vessels and not used to the kind of risks involved in battle. That night, Nelson sent Captain Thomas Hardy out in a boat to take soundings round the Danish position. Despite his reputation for making headlong and risky attacks, Nelson was meticulous on this occasion.

Around 9.30am on 2 April the ships began to weigh anchor and set sail on a southerly breeze. Two, the *Bellona* and the *Russell*, went aground on the shoal but within an hour the leading ship,

ABOVE
The Battle of Copenhagen, 2 April 1801. *Nelson is in the Elephant, 74 guns, flying his blue vice-admiral's flag (centre left). Bomb vessels in the foreground anchored on the edge of the Middle Ground shoal, shell the inshore defences. By Nicholas Pocock.*

RIGHT
Captain Edward Riou (1758-1801). He commanded the frigates at Copenhagen in the Amazon, 38, and was killed there. A miniature by Samuel Shelley (c. 1750-1808)

Vincent, believed that the blockading force should be stationed almost permanently off the enemy port, leaving only when forced to by extreme weather. The other school, led by Lord Howe, argued that this put unnecessary strain on ships and men and allowed the enemy to choose his moment to attack; the port should be watched by frigates, while the main fleet remained alert but safe in harbour. Historians have generally favoured St Vincent's approach, the close blockade, against Howe's open block-ade. Nelson's blockade of Toulon was somewhere between the two. This was partly because he had no suitable base for his fleet. Britain now held Malta but that could be several weeks sailing from Toulon and was not favoured by Nelson. Instead he used an anchorage in the Maddalena Islands north of Sardinia as an advanced base, despite its insecurity. Rather than detach a few ships there at a time, he generally kept his ships of the line together and withdrew them as a body. Captain Whitby complained in 1804:

Though Lord Nelson is indefatigable in keeping the sea, there are so many reasons that make it possible for the French to escape through the Mediterranean.... First, he does not cruise upon his rendezvous; second-ly, I have consequently known him from a week to three weeks, and even a month, unfound by ships sent to reconnoitre.... Thirdly he is occasionally obliged to take the whole squadron to water, a great distance from Toulon; fourthly, since I came away the French squadron got out in his absence, and cruised off Toulon several days, and at last when he came out, he only got sight of them at a great distance, to see them arrive at their own harbour.[11]

The main point in favour of Nelson's system was that an overly tight blockade would never entice the enemy out to be destroyed. In this way, the French Brest fleet remained in harbour for the rest of the war as a 'fleet in being', while the

THE GREAT CHASE

In May 1803, as war with France resumed, Nelson was given command of the Medi-terranean fleet, with his flag in the *Victory*. He arrived on station off Toulon on 8 July to find nine ships of the line, one frigate and one sloop. His main task was to blockade the French Mediterranean fleet in Toulon. There were two main schools of thought on the conduct of blockades. The more aggressive, headed by St

'Buonaparte hearing of Nelson's Victory swears by his Sword to Extirpate the English from off of the Earth.' *Napoleon's fury after the Battle of the Nile. He proclaimed himself emperor in 1804 but Nelson never called him anything more complimentary than 'General Bonaparte' or 'the Corsican scoundrel'. By James Gillray.*

AN ACCURATE REPRESENTATION of the FLOATING MACHINE Invented by the FRENCH for INVADING ENGLAND. and Acts on the principals of both Wind & Water Mills. carries 60-000 Men & 600 Cannon.

Toulon squadron was eventually destroyed. Brest was also much closer to Britain than Toulon. If the Toulon fleet escaped, it would have to travel for several weeks before it could really damage British interests and if it left the Mediterranean it would probably be detected from Gibraltar.

The French were determined to escape, for early in 1805 Napoleon conceived a far-reaching plan for invasion. The separate French and Spanish fleets were to elude their blockaders and sail for the West Indies. Having distracted the British and caused the Navy to disperse its forces in search of them, they would unite and sail back across the Atlantic, taking control of the English Channel and supporting an invasion of Britain. The Toulon fleet, under Admiral Villeneuve, actually escaped once while Nelson was at Maddalena but put back again owing to bad weather. Nelson, ignorant of this, had returned to Egypt in search of them. Villeneuve got out again on 30 March and Nelson received the news while watering his ship at Maddalena.

Thus began another epic chase, with even greater potential consequences than that of 1798:

Between 1803 and 1805 Napoleon built up a Grande Armée of 130,000 men around Boulogne, to invade Britain. This nightmarish invasion barge is one of many paranoid fantasies for which printsellers found a ready market. The 2,300 real barges were more conventional, much smaller and never used.

failure would result in the invasion of Britain rather than Egypt and India. Although Nelson's role was vital, he was no longer the principal player as he had been at the Nile. The British strategy involved several different fleets and was very effectively co-ordinated by Charles Middleton, now Lord Barham and First Lord of the Admiralty.

This did not make Nelson's decisions any easier. As in 1798, the enemy could have gone anywhere and he eventually discovered that they had passed through the Straits of Gibraltar. By that time, he was six weeks behind Villeneuve. Later he heard that they had gone to the West Indies and followed them there. He made up much lost time and on 4 June was at Barbados, only 100 miles from the French at Martinique. False intelligence caused him to go south to St Lucia and the chance of battle was missed, for by 12 June Nelson was certain that the enemy had gone back across the Atlantic.

Captain Bettesworth of the brig *Curieux* was sent to England to brief Lord Barham, who then mobilized his forces. The Admiralty had never dispersed its ships as the French had hoped and strong squadrons remained off the enemy ports. Sir Robert Calder, off Ferrol in Spain, was ordered to deploy his forces to intercept the returning French, which he did successfully. On 22 July, with 15 ships of the line, he met Villeneuve with 20. The action was fought in poor weather and Calder captured two enemy ships. Ten years earlier Hotham had been rewarded for less but attitudes had changed since then. Instead of being honoured, Calder was eventually court-martialled and reprimanded; Nelson's example had taught the public and the Admiralty to expect nothing less than annihilation of the enemy. Strategically, Calder's action was successful, for Napoleon abandoned his invasion plans;

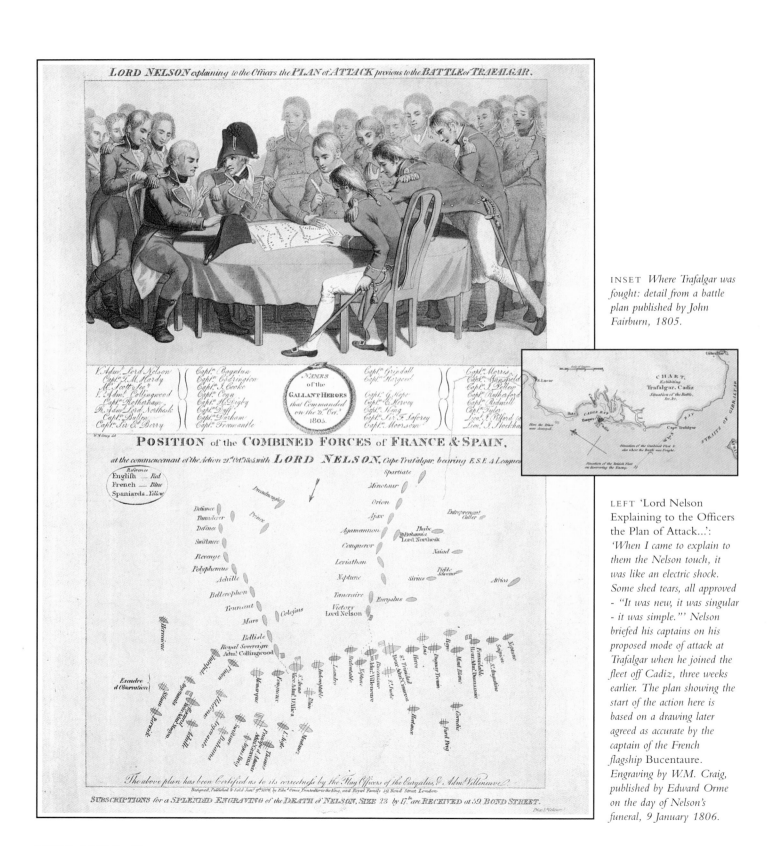

INSET *Where Trafalgar was fought: detail from a battle plan published by John Fairburn, 1805.*

LEFT 'Lord Nelson Explaining to the Officers the Plan of Attack...': *'When I came to explain to them the Nelson touch, it was like an electric shock. Some shed tears, all approved - "It was new, it was singular - it was simple."'* Nelson briefed his captains on his proposed mode of attack at Trafalgar when he joined the fleet off Cadiz, three weeks earlier. The plan showing the start of the action here is based on a drawing later agreed as accurate by the captain of the French flagship Bucentaure. Engraving by W.M. Craig, published by Edward Orme on the day of Nelson's funeral, 9 January 1806.

in August he struck the Boulogne camp and marched his troops off on a campaign against Austria.

Nelson arrived back at Gibraltar on 19 July and returned to England a month later. Early in September he was told that the combined Franco-Spanish fleet had put into Cadiz. Within a fortnight he had re-hoisted his flag aboard the *Victory* and sailed to take command of the fleet blockading that port.

TRAFALGAR

In normal circumstances, there was no reason to expect the Combined Fleet to come out and fight, and Nelson's blockade of Cadiz might have become a long tale of endurance and patience, punctuated by daring raids on enemy shore positions. But Napoleon goaded Villeneuve with accusations of cowardice, ordering him to sail into the Mediterranean and support the French armies in southern Italy. On 19 October the Combined Fleet began the long operation of raising its anchors and leaving port. The following morning 33 French and Spanish ships of the line, with five frigates and two brigs, were steering out of Cadiz into the open sea.

Nelson was well informed of the enemy movements by his watching frigates. As always he was confident of victory, though his fleet of 27 of the line and 4 frigates was smaller than he had expected. He had planned for a force of 40 ships, but several had been detached or had not yet joined. His original plan had been to divide the fleet into three squadrons. One was to cut the enemy line a third of the way from its head. A second was to engage and capture the larger body of ships which were thus cut off. The third part, the 'advanced squadron', under 'an officer who, I am sure, will employ them in the manner I wish, if possible'[12], was to intervene as the situation

Sir Henry Blackwood, Vice-Admiral of the White (1770-1832). At Trafalgar he commanded the frigates, in the Euryalus, *but until the first shots were fired was aboard* Victory *where he witnessed Nelson's last will. 'God bless you Blackwood', Nelson replied to his parting good wishes, 'I shall never speak to you again.' By John Hoppner (1758-1810).*

The Trafalgar telescope of John Pasco, Victory's *signal lieutenant. When Nelson said he wanted to hoist 'England* confides *that every man will do his duty', Pasco asked to use 'expects', which needed fewer flags. 'That will do', said Nelson, 'make it directly.'*

developed. In the event, Nelson was short of ships and attacked with his fleet divided into two parallel columns. The windward column led by himself in the *Victory*, was to cut the enemy line at the fleet flagship in the centre. The leeward squadron, under his old friend Collingwood in the *Royal Sovereign*, was to engage the rear part of the enemy. Thus, their centre and rear would be overwhelmed before the van could turn and assist.

At dawn on 21 October 1805, the Franco-Spanish fleet saw the British for the first time, and Villeneuve decided he would rather fight under the shelter of Cadiz. He ordered his ships

Cuthbert Collingwood, Baron Collingwood, Vice-Admiral of the Red (1750-1810). Nelson's 'dear Coll' was a quiet Northumbrian and they began a lifelong friendship as lieutenants in the West Indies. As captain of the Excellent, 74 guns, he distinguished himself at Cape St Vincent and in 1799 took over the Channel Fleet as a rear-admiral. He was second-in-command at Trafalgar in the Royal Sovereign, 100 guns, and on Nelson's death remained in command of the Mediterranean Fleet. He never saw England again, dying on the way home. A posthumous portrait by Henry Howard (1769-1847).

Blackwood told Nelson that he thought the capture of 14 of the enemy would be a good haul; Nelson said he would not be satisfied with less than 20. Sailors talked about how much prize money they would make and how long the war would last after the battle. On the other side all was gloom and despair. No one expected to win, least of all Villeneuve. He was well aware that his men were ill-trained from months in harbour, that they had none of the tactical skill of Nelson's fleet and that their gunnery and seamanship were woefully inadequate against the world's most feared admiral.

Collingwood reached the enemy line first, and around noon the Royal Sovereign began to engage with the Spanish Santa Ana. The Victory was in action soon afterwards and the battle became general within the hour, as the other ships came up and chose their targets. Soon a mêlée developed, with ships engaging one or two of the enemy. It was a hot fight at close range and Nelson remarked to his flag-captain, 'This is too warm work, Hardy, to last long.' Shortly after

to wear round, thus reversing their course and order and causing some confusion in their line. Progress was slow in light winds and Nelson's ships, especially the leading ones, were at greatest risk as they approached the enemy line at right angles, exposing their bows to the full broadsides of the enemy. His judgement of the Combined Fleet's gunnery was correct, however: it was not good enough to do real damage at this stage.

During the approach Nelson made his most famous signal, 'England expects that every man will do his duty', and the mood aboard the British ships was one of great confidence, despite the enemy's superiority in numbers. Captain

Trafalgar, 21 October 1805: the start of the action, from the north-east. Almost in the centre, the Victory rakes Admiral Villeneuve's flagship Bucentaure from astern as she breaks from right to left through the Franco-Spanish line, at the head of Nelson's weather division. In the distance Collingwood's Royal Sovereign and the lee division are already closely engaged. By Nicholas Pocock.

1pm, Nelson was shot by a marksman in the mizzen top of the French *Redoutable* and taken below, where he died later in the afternoon. The action continued and by the end of the day 18 enemy ships had escaped, with 15 surrendered. All but four of these were lost in the storm that followed the battle, the end of which was marked at about 5pm by a massive explosion as the French 74, *Achille*, blew up after catching fire.

Trafalgar was perhaps the most famous sea battle ever fought. It was the only one of Nelson's three great actions which took place in the open sea, against ships which were sailing rather than at anchor. It gained dramatic effect because of the death of Nelson and because it was the last in the long series of major battles, going back over a century, between Britain and France. As a victory it has notable statistical significance; it was the only great battle in which large numbers of ships were captured despite the victors' considerable numerical inferiority. It also confirmed the superiority of British seapower for a further century.

For the war as a whole it had rather less significance. Napoleon had already abandoned his invasion plans, so it did not alter the real balance of power in the way that the Nile had done. It did not end the naval war, which continued for almost another ten years, nor did it destroy the French navy. This soon built new ships and remained an intermittent threat to British seapower for the rest of the nineteenth century. In some ways the legend of Trafalgar was greater than the reality but its long-term effect on public opinion and on naval tradition was decisive.

THE NELSON TOUCH

Despite his great success in fleet battles, there is little evidence that Nelson thought much about naval tactics as a science. He summed up his basic philosophy in 1803:

The French Achille, *74 guns, caught fire at Trafalgar and blew up afterwards. British boats rescued survivors including a young woman called Jeannette, found clinging naked to a spar. She had been aboard disguised as a man to be with her husband, with whom she was reunited among the prisoners. At least one other woman, probably more, was present on the British side. This prints dates to 1817.*

The business of a commander-in-chief being first to bring an enemy's fleet to battle on the most advantageous terms to himself (I mean that of laying his ships close on board the enemy, as expeditiously as possible, and secondly to continue them there without separating until the issue is decided). I am sensible beyond this object it is not necessary that I should say a word, being fully assured that the admirals and captains of the fleet I have the honour to command will, knowing my precise object, that of a close and decisive battle, supply any deficiency of my making signals.[13]

The success of these tactics depended on two factors; the demoralization of the enemy and Nelson's own charisma and skill. It was dangerous to follow his principles slavishly if these elements were not present. He placed great emphasis on close-range gunnery and a high rate of fire, at the expense of accuracy. In 1814 Sir Howard Douglas was in a bombardment of the shore and the low standard of accuracy made him 'tremble for the laurels of the Navy'. Of course, Nelson had many other positive effects on the Navy; he developed the tradition of victory, the high

RIGHT *The fall of Nelson. At about 1.30pm Nelson and Captain Hardy were pacing the* Victory's *quarterdeck. Hardy turned and saw Nelson collapsing on deck saying 'They have done for me at last... my backbone is shot through'; he died about three hours later. By Denis Dighton (1792-1827).*

ABOVE The Battle of Trafalgar, *by Joseph Mallord William Turner (1775-1851). Turner's only royal commission, ordered by George IV in 1822. It combines a series of incidents into an evocation of events which displeased most naval officers and proved highly controversial when it was delivered in 1824 to form a pair with de Loutherbourg's* Glorious First of June *(see page 52). In 1829 the King gave both pictures to Greenwich Hospital.* Victory *is shown losing her foretopmast.*

Nelson's Trafalgar coat. The bullet hole is in the left shoulder of this, a flag-officer's 1795-1812 undress coat, with Nelson's various orders sewn on: the star of the Order of Bath, the Turkish Order of the Crescent, the cross of the German Chapteral Order of St Joachim and the Neapolitan Order of St Ferdinand and of Merit.

'The Bullet by which Nelson was Killed': the French musket ball, ⅝in (1.5cm) in diameter, which Dr Beatty removed from Nelson's body. The indentation was caused by impact with bone. Beatty had the locket (above) made to preserve the ball and the fragments of Nelson's epaulette which it carried in its path. In 1842 his family presented it to Queen Victoria.

morale and the refusal to accept anything less than complete victory.

There have been virtually no decisive surface-ship fleet actions since Nelson's death. A notable exception, very much in the Nelsonic tradition, was the annihilation of the Russian Baltic fleet by Admiral Togo's Japanese fleet at the Battle of Tsushima in 1905, the centenary of Trafalgar. The last real sailing ship battle was the easy defeat of the Turks by the French and British at Navarino in 1827. The Battle of Jutland in 1916 employed a different technology and proved a

The Death of Nelson in Victory's cockpit, by Arthur William Devis (1763-1822). Captain Hardy stands over him with Walter Burke, the purser, by the pillow; Nelson's steward, Chevalier, looks at Dr Beatty who feels for the pulse. On the left the Revd Alexander Scott, Nelson's chaplain and secretary, finally stops rubbing his chest to relieve the pain.

terrible disappointment to those who thought that the spirit of Nelson would always succeed in the British navy. The German fleet was not elim-inated: indeed, more British ships were lost than German. The Nelson myth was very important in the 1914-18 war, for the public and the Navy. Both, however, overestimated what the fleet could achieve and the public failed to understand that 'Nelsonic victories' were no longer possible in the age of steel, steam, torpedoes and sub-marines, or against efficient modern enemies.

The end of the Battle of Trafalgar. Victory *is in the centre with only her foremast standing and the dismasted and captured* Bucentaure *beyond. Astern of her Collingwood's* Royal Sovereign, *also with only a foremast, lies beside the captured Spanish three-decker* Santa Ana. *The row of three ships, bow on to their right, are the British* Temeraire *between her two French prizes,* Redoutable *and* Fougueux. *By Nicholas Pocock, this is a pair to his view of the start of the action (see page 108); both were engraved in Nelson's 1809 biography.*

'NO COMMON BEING': NELSON'S CHARACTER AND RELATIONSHIPS

FOR those who look back on Nelson's career, through a perspective long distorted by myth and reverence, what may seem most striking is the contrast between his calm dedication to the greater good of his country and the calculating dynamism he focused on the destruction of its enemies. This image is inherited from more overtly nationalistic times and the artists and writers who created it were, of course, reproducing Nelson as they wanted the public to see him: as a man above the more sordid problems of lesser mortals, patriotic, all-comprehending, supremely powerful through the gifts and authority vested in him, vengeful yet protective. This combination of attributes, with its implications of divine inspiration, is the portrait of an imperial hero.

The received impression is still strong, for in some respects it is also true. Nelson was without doubt intelligent, energetic, highly patriotic and aggressive. But he was not free of familiar personal problems and had traits which many contemporaries regarded as flaws, as we would today. To naval officers used to concealing 'unmanly' feeling, he was unduly emotional. To others, conscious of the qualities needed for high military office, he seemed pretentious. Like most human beings, he wanted approval: affection from those he loved, practical rewards from those he served and public honours from those placed to bestow them. The Crown, in particular, he came to revere with near-religious devotion. Above all, he was motivated by ambition: both to achieve the highest accolades open to him and to find fulfilment in his personal life.

A miniature believed to show Nelson at the age of eight. Artist unknown.

EARLY INFLUENCES

When considering how this personality was shaped, it is important to remember that Nelson was the third of five boys, in a brood of eight children born to a country parson of no wealth and few useful connections. From the first, he had to fight for his social survival. His mother probably had only limited time to give him her affection and died when Nelson was nine. Thereafter he was subject to boarding and day schools where flogging was regarded as normal discipline and to the kindly but uncertain guidance of his ineffective father. Edmund Nelson must have convinced his son of the benefits of making up his own mind and asserting his own opinion, a habit developed in his career and in his prolific correspondence. The impressions of these early days remained

Nelson's mother, Catherine Suckling (1725-67). This copy of a painting by J. T. Heins (1697-1756) shows her at the age of eighteen.

with him all his life. In 1804, assuming he would be buried with his father at Burnham Thorpe, he admitted that 'the thought of former days brings all my mother to my heart, which shows itself in my eyes'[1]

This upbringing gave Nelson's character a mixture of sentiment and determination, as contemporaries were aware. A protégé, Sir George Cockburn, recalled him as 'always a curious compound of weakness, with power of high exertions of intrepidity and talent whenever great occasions called for the exertion of the nobler qualities and the subjection of the former'.[2] Lord Minto put it more bluntly five weeks before Nelson died: 'He is in many points a really great man, in others a baby.'[3] Both men liked Nelson. Cockburn was impressed with his 'never failing kindness of heart.' Lord Malmesbury liked his 'kindness and

thoughtfulness' so much as to 'even forgive his foibles in favour of his goodness of heart'.[4]

One vehicle for both the emotional and ambitious sides of Nelson's nature was religion, the forms of which he had learnt at Burnham Thorpe. After his vision of a 'radiant orb' at the age of seventeen, when he entrusted himself to providence and resolved to be a hero, his commitment to the service of Britain became an article of faith. His last prayer, written on the morning of Trafalgar, could well have come direct from a pulpit:

May the Great God whom I worship, Grant to my Country and for the benefit of Europe in General a great and Glorious Victory and may no misconduct in anyone tarnish it, and May humanity after Victory be the predominant feature in the British fleet. For myself individually I commit my Life to Him who made me,

and may his blessing light upon my endeavours for serving my Country faithfully, to Him I resign myself and the Just cause which is entrusted to me to defend – Amen, Amen, Amen.'[5] This inner commitment conveyed itself in his attitude and manner to his friends. Lord Minto observed after his death: 'there was a heroic cast about Nelson that I never saw in any other man, and which seems wanting to the achievement of impossible things.'[6]

NELSON'S PHILOSOPHY

This heroic cast was certainly related to Nelson's awareness of the risk of death or mutilation in achieving 'impossible things'. Before the Battle of the Nile he was sure he would return 'either crowned with laurel or covered with cypress'[7]. He constantly strove for the laurel but explained

The Revd Edmund Nelson (1722-1802). Nelson's wife, Fanny, persuaded Sir William Beechey to come and paint Nelson's father in 1800 when the old man was too frail to visit the artist's studio.

the fatalistic aspect of his philosophy to his wife, Fanny, in 1795:

Whatever may be my fate, I have no doubt in my own mind but that my conduct will be such as will not bring a blush on the face of my friends: the lives of all are in the hands of Him, who knows best whether to preserve mine or not; to his will do I resign myself. My character and good name are in my own keeping. Life with disgrace is dreadful. A glorious death is to be envied; and, if anything happens to me, recollect that death is a debt we must all pay, and whether now or a few years hence can be but of little consequence.[8]

This firm course to death or glory gave Nelson a goal higher than material attainments. It carried him through the setbacks, hardships and frustrations of both naval and personal life with some sense of destiny. It also expressed his devotion, enthusiasm and the sense of anticipation he derived from his career. Less positively, it tended to make him self-absorbed and prone to ignoring his obligations to others – an unfortunate trait in someone who, from his earliest days in the Navy, owed others a great deal.

His intense and exceptional pursuit of self-fulfilment was, then, a two-edged sword. Professionally it brought him both acclaim and disrepute; in his private life it brought him brief periods of happiness but longer ones of great misery. Those who knew him were aware of his problems, his volatility and mood swings. Charm, courage and success seemed to redeem him but he was not generally a happy man except when at sea, preoccupied with the war and his duties and surrounded by others similarly divorced from domestic society.

CONSTRAINTS AND BONDS

Nelson's unhappy cast of mind was reinforced by his life as a successful seaman, which separated him from shore society for much of the time. Its first effect was in limiting the people with whom he could become intimate to those he met in relatively short periods ashore. His emotional involvements with both Frances Nisbet, whom he married, and later Emma Hamilton, arose from this channelled social life. Neither were entirely suitable as objects of his affections. The second effect was to make him dependent for many of his friendships on a service structure that was in some ways predatory. In the Navy, personal relationships were permeated by professional ones. Rarely could officers care for each other as equals, for rank and seniority made all men either superior or subordinate to each other. Every superior was influential, every subordinate subject to command, in a relationship that could enhance or compromise efficiency. Most of Nelson's close naval relationships were either with potential patrons or with clients aware of what he could do for them. That he engendered intense loyalty from, and did have genuine friendships with, a largely junior 'band of brothers' was one of the most remarkable things about him as a personality and a commander.

Socially constrained within his private and professional life, Nelson nevertheless quickly learnt how to achieve his social goals. In the process he had to shrug off many earlier inhibitions including those derived from home. He was clearly very fond of his family, as shown in one of his few surviving early letters to his father:

When I reach New York you shall hear what becomes of me; but whilst I have health it is indifferent to me (were it not for the pleasure of seeing you and my brothers and sisters) where I go....If Nanny or Kate are with you, give my kind love to them, and to all as you write to them.[9]

His father's letters in return were pious in the extreme, as one of 1793 shows:

Every mark of my affection you may justly expect; and it gives me satisfaction to reflect on the many proofs I have had of your disposition to observe those duties which each relation in life calls for. The approbation of your own mind is far more pleasing than any supposed partiality of mine; though a reward infinitely short of what moral virtue, which is an attendant on true religion, shall one day receive. The principal domestic occurrence at this juncture is that of your brother's ordination....[10]

After the death of Nelson's mother, it was natural for his father to act as his moral guide, which was perhaps more a disadvantage than a benefit. Such guidance from home can only have reinforced the strait-jacket of his early moral upbringing. His marriage to someone of Frances Nisbet's quiet, well-bred and unadventurous nature was therefore understandable; so too the eruption of passion over Emma Hamilton and, once his own emotional restraints were broken, the anger at the social comment it created.

The early bonds were maintained the longer because at heart Nelson was a kind man, as revealed in his steady and affectionate correspondence with his older brother, William. He rightly judged William timid, unadventurous and irritating, partly because he always seemed in hopes of benefitting from Nelson's advancement. Yet Nelson always remained kind, perhaps because of an element of admiration in William's regard for him. After ordination William briefly hankered to become a naval chaplain. In 1784, Nelson took him to the West Indies in the *Boreas* but, after the voyage out, William soon returned home sick. Nelson's kindness had its return. William remained loyal after the breakdown of Nelson's marriage. He and his family provided support for Emma and the Merton household, while his daughter, Charlotte, stayed with Emma and Nelson and gave them a real sense of domesticity at the time they most needed it.

Mrs Mary Moutray (1753–c.1840), wife of the much older dockyard commissioner at Antigua and warm friend to both Nelson and Collingwood. After she returned to England and was widowed it was Collingwood rather than Nelson who remained her steadiest correspondent. A portrait drawing by John Downman (1750–1824).

For Nelson, families were about social and economic support as well as affection. He was fortunate in having two uncles, brothers of his mother, who were both of practical value to him. While Captain Maurice Suckling provided for his entry to the Navy and early advancement, William Suckling was a potential source of money when he needed it.

EARLY AFFECTIONS

But family relations did not provide all that a young naval officer demanded. Nelson was always interested in women and they always had an interest in him. Whenever the opportunity offered, before he married, Nelson's affections regularly focused on attractive young women, the more intently after long periods at sea. He first fell in love in 1781 at the age of twenty-three, when at Quebec. Mary Simpson, the daughter of the garrison Provost-Marshal, was only sixteen. She found him correct and stern but charming. Nelson's imagination quickly ran riot, immediately jumping to thoughts of marriage. On the point of departure in October he almost proposed but was prevented from doing so by Alexander Davison, a friend in whom he had confided. The infatuation seems to have been quickly forgotten. Late in 1783 he was again greatly smitten, while staying at St Omer in France with Captain James Macnamara. The two young men played cards nightly with the two vivacious daughters of their landlady but this pleasure palled with the arrival of a Mr Andrews, a clergyman, and his daughters. Nelson was quickly convinced of the 'accomplishments' of one of them and began spending much of his time with her. By January 1784, back in England, he felt committed to raising money to support a proposal of marriage. Desperate, he wrote to William Suckling for a yearly allowance:

The critical moment of my life is now arrived that either I am to be happy or miserable – it depends solely on you. You may possibly think I am going to ask too much. I have led myself up with hopes you will not – till this trying moment. There is a lady I have seen, of a good family and connexions, but with a small fortune – £1000 I understand. The whole of my income does not exceed £130 per annum. Now I must come to the point: will you, if I should marry, allow me yearly £100 until my income is increased to that sum, either by employment or any other way? A very few years I hope would turn something up, if my friends will but exert themselves. If you will not give me the above sum, will you exert yourself with either Lord North or Mr Jenkinson to get me a guardship or some employment in a public office…? You must excuse the freedom with which this letter is dictated; not to have been plain and explicit in my distress had been cruel to myself. If nothing can be done for me, I know what I have to trust to. Life is not worth preserving without happiness; and I care not where I may linger out a miserable existence.[11]

His uncle agreed to help but in the event this was not necessary: Miss Andrews was not ready for marriage. Nelson's affections could not wait, however. Later that year, as captain of the *Boreas* in the West Indies, he met Mary Moutray. At thirty-two, she was six years older than Nelson, and already married to the Commissioner John Moutray at Antigua. She was loyal and loving, and had borne her husband two children, but the Commissioner was almost thirty years older and

Mary clearly found her friendships with younger visiting captains a relief from the tedium of island life. Nelson enjoyed her company for the same reason: 'Was it not for Mrs Moutray, who is very very good to me, I should hang myself at this infernal hole,' he wrote.[12] The relationship was to survive; in February 1785 he wrote to his brother, William:

You may be certain I never passed English harbour without a call, but alas! I am not to have much comfort. My dear, sweet friend is going home. I am really an April day; happy on her account, but truly grieved were I only to consider myself. Her equal I never saw in any country or in any situation.[13]

When they finally parted, Nelson took his leave 'with a heavy heart.… What a treasure of a woman. God bless her.'[14] He was not the only officer fond of Mary Moutray. His close friend Cuthbert Collingwood, who was on the same station, had carried the Moutrays out to the West Indies. Collingwood was also a regular guest at the Commissioner's house and was, if anything, closer to Mary than Nelson. Nelson declared he would miss them grievously: 'she is quite a delight and makes many an hour cheerful that without her would be dead weight'.[15] He kept up a spasmodic correspondence with Mary for the rest of his life.

MARRIAGE

Nelson soon found other consolation. On the neighbouring island of Nevis there was a widow only a few months older than himself, who acted as hostess for her rich uncle on his sugar estate of Montpelier. Only on his third visit, in the spring of 1785, did he meet Frances Nisbet, who had already heard the following description of him from a friend:

We have at last seen the little captain of the Boreas, of whom so much has been said. He came up just before

Frances, Viscountess Nelson (1761-1831). Nelson's wife, by an unknown artist.

dinner, much heated and was very silent yet seemed, according to the old adage, to think the more. He declined drinking any wine: but after dinner, when the president, as usual, has the three following toasts, the King, the Queen, and the Royal Family, and Lord Hood, this strange man regularly filled his glass and observed that those were always bumper toasts with him; which having drank, he uniformly passed the bottle and relapsed into his former taciturnity. It was impossible, during this visit, for any of us to make out his real character; there was such a reserve and sternness in his behaviour, with occasional sallies, though very transient, of a superior mind. Being placed by him, I endeavoured to rouse his attention by showing him all the civilities in my power: but I drew out little more than yes and no. If you, Fanny, had been there, we

think you would have made something of him; for you have been in the habit of attending to these odd sort of people.[16]

Fanny and Nelson did seem to hit it off, possibly because Nelson enjoyed playing with her son, Josiah. By August 1785 he was already hoping that her uncle would permit their marriage:

Most fervently do I hope his answer will be of such a tendency as to convey real pleasure not only to myself but also to you, for most sincerely do I love you and I trust that my affection is not only founded upon the principles of reason but also upon the basis of mutual attachment. Indeed, my charming Fanny, did I possess a million my greatest pride and pleasure would be to share it with you; and, as I am, to live in a cottage with you I should esteem superior to living in a palace with any other I have yet met with. My age is enough to make me seriously reflect what I have offered and common sense tells me what a good choice I have made. The more I weigh you in my mind, the more reason I find to admire both your head and heart.[17]

Sincere affection, esteem, reason and mutual attachment formed the basis of their marriage; but Nelson was also interested in the financial provision Fanny's uncle would make for her and what he could obtain from a sympathetic William Suckling. 'I know the way to get him to give me most is not to appear to want it,' he wrote to Suckling in November; 'thus circumstanced, who can I apply to but you? My future happiness, I give you my honour, is now in your power.... Don't disappoint me or my heart will break.... I... trust implicitly to your goodness, and pray let me know of your generous action by the first packet.'[18]

Nelson was clumsy in his expressions of affection to Fanny but a date for the wedding was fixed in March 1787 to allow Prince William Henry to give her away. Returning to England separately, the couple were reunited in London and, after visiting friends and relations, they settled down in Burnham Thorpe.

As they really got to know one another Nelson found himself dominating the housekeeping as well as farming his father's church lands. Fanny found the winters too cold and the lack of society irksome. It was a tiresome six years. Children might have made a difference but they remained childless. When he returned to sea in 1793 Nelson did not refrain from revealing his irritation at Fanny's inefficiency in managing his practical requirements. Clumsiness now developed into rudeness but they maintained a regular and dutiful correspondence which was a support to them both. Nelson's letters to Fanny frequently expressed his growing confidence as a fighting

officer; hers just as frequently showed her anxiety for his health and safety. Though their letters began and ended in terms of affection, and were full of common knowledge, his boldness clashed with her timidity. When opportunities offered for returning home, Nelson preferred to remain where there was activity, excitement and prospects of promotion. In 1797, when he lost his arm and finally returned home, Fanny nursed him tenderly. They had been apart for four years and for her these few weeks were perhaps the happiest and most fulfilling of their married life. On his return to sea in March 1798, however, Nelson's old irritation with her inefficiency resumed.

During those four years at sea, though never disclosed to Fanny, there was at least one other woman in his life. At Leghorn in 1794-5, Nelson regularly entertained on board an opera singer, Adelaide Correglia. A surviving note appeals to her 'to think of him always'. Fremantle, a brother captain, observed disapprovingly in the summer of 1795: 'Dined with Nelson. Dolly aboard... he makes himself ridiculous with that woman.'[19]

THE PASSION OF HIS LIFE

By this time Nelson had also met Emma Hamilton, whom he commended to Fanny in 1793 as having been 'wonderfully kind and good' to Josiah, Fanny's son by her first marriage, who was with Nelson in the *Agamemnon*. She was 'a young woman of amiable manners' who did 'honour to the station to which she is raised'.[20] Her chequered background seems to have been known to him, for she was probably a subject of gossip. He also liked Sir William Hamilton, with whom he necessarily corresponded. Hamilton was sixty-seven in 1798, more than thirty years older than his exuberant young wife. Emma's

Emma, Lady Hamilton (c.1761-1815) as a Bacchante, by Louise-Elizabeth Vigée-Le Brun (1755-1842). This role, as one of the attendants of the Roman god of wine, was among those adopted by Emma in her celebrated 'attitudes'. This was one of several pictures of her painted at Naples in the years 1790-2 by Mme Vigée-Le Brun who wrote: 'She had a great quantity of beautiful chestnut hair which could cover her entirely and as a bacchante, with her hair spread out, she was admirable.'

EMMA

Amy Lyon was the daughter of a Cheshire blacksmith, who died in 1765, when she may have been as old as four. As Emily or Emma Hart she went into domestic service in London, then almost certainly into prostitution. In 1780 she had a child, Emma, who was later fostered and died in about 1804, and then became mistress of Sir Harry Fetherstonhaugh of Uppark, who threw her out before she gave birth to another child, probably stillborn. She was rescued by the Hon. Charles Greville, possibly the child's father; he educated her among friends including artists such as Romney and Reynolds, who painted his beautiful and good-humoured mistress. In 1784 Greville introduced her to his uncle Sir William Hamilton and in 1786, to reduce his own expenses, 'passed her on' to Hamilton in Naples, with her mother. She was initially furious but became an instant social success, rapidly learnt Italian (with a Lancashire accent), sang wonderfully, and gained wide fame by her 'attitudes' - one-woman tableau-vivant performances. Hamilton doted on her: they became lovers and in 1791 married in London. On return to Naples as the ambassador's wife, she was presented to Queen Maria-Carolina, of whom she soon became a close friend and confidante.

Nelson met Emma in 1793 but it was after the Nile that her extravagant hero-worship sparked off a mutual passion - reinforced by the events of the Neapolitan revolt, in which she showed great courage. Though still handsome she was already very fat with the easy manner of a barmaid, according to Lord Minto. The affair became the scandal of the Mediterranean and of fashionable London when the Hamiltons and Nelson returned there in 1800. Emma was then pregnant with Nelson's daughter Horatia, born early in 1801, shortly before Nelson finally left his

One of a pair of pastel portraits of Nelson and Emma by Johann Schmidt (1749-1828), Court Painter to the Elector of Saxony. They were done at Dresden in 1800 during their overland return to England.

Nelson afterwards had this in his cabin at sea. Emma wrote on the back: 'He called it his "Guardian Angel" and thought he could not be victorious if he could not see it in the midst of Battle....'

BELOW *Emma in an attitude: an engraving from the series, of 1794, which Sir William commissioned from* the German artist Frederick Rehberg to record his wife's drawing-room performances.

Trimming from a dress worn by Lady Hamilton at a fête in Palermo in 1799, with oak leaves embroidered around Nelson's name and Sicilian ducal title.

wife. A second daughter died aged two or three months in March 1804. The death of Sir William in 1803, and of Nelson, left Emma moderately well provided for. Her grief for Nelson was as public as her adoration but his last request for a pension for her was ignored. Always spendthrift, she soon ran into debt for which she was imprisoned in 1813. On release she went to live in Calais with Horatia where, drinking heavily, she died in January 1815.

response to Nelson's arrival that year in search of the French was charged with excitement and emotion. On hearing of the victory at the Nile she was ecstatic and fainted with joy.

Suffering from a head wound as well as a bout of malaria, Nelson readily accepted the invitation to recuperate in the Hamiltons' house at Naples and there, from 22 September 1798, he rapidly fell under Emma's overwhelming spell. 'She is one of the very best women in the world,' he told Fanny on his arrival. 'How few could have made the turn she has. She is an honour to her sex and proof that even reputation may be regained, but I own it requires a great soul.'[21] To mark his birthday on 29 September the Hamiltons held a great ball, magnificent in theatrical celebration of his victory. Mainly, however, they cared for him, providing the relaxation of their palazzo and villas with, on the one hand, the stimulation of intelligent conversation and, on the other, of a motherly, voluptuous and flirtatious affection. 'I am writing opposite Lady Hamilton,' he told St Vincent, his stern commander-in-chief, early in October, 'therefore you will not be surprised at the glorious jumble of this letter. Were your Lordship in my place, I much doubt if you could write so well; our hearts and our hands must be all in a flutter.'[22]

Merton Place: a drawing of 1802, by Thomas Baxter, of the house which Emma found for Nelson after their return from Naples. The bridge, right, spans the artificial canal where Sir William fished and which they called 'the Nile'. The house was demolished in 1846.

Nelson's visiting card, the combined knife and fork he used after the loss of his arm and one of his left-hand kid gloves, with his name written in the cuff by Lady Hamilton.

As he regained his strength, Nelson naturally began to take an interest in the security of Naples, inevitably influenced by his new affection. He regularly met King Ferdinand of the Two Sicilies, Queen Maria Carolina and their half-English Prime Minister, Sir John Acton, who awaited an invasion by the French from Rome, which they already held. Nelson urged an offensive by Ferdinand's troops, with his fleet's support, but the plan backfired and the French counter-attacked. Over Christmas, Nelson evacuated the Neapolitan royal family and the Hamiltons to Palermo, where Emma and Nelson became sexually involved.

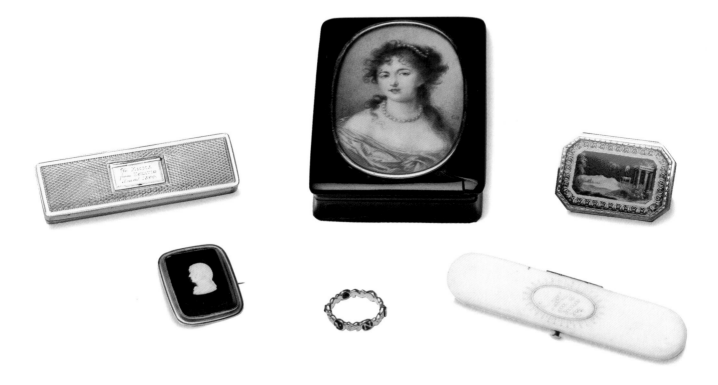

For Nelson, the power of the emotions that were aroused was enhanced by ill-health and by the lack of any previous experience to compare with it. In April, when Naples seemed on the point of recapture from the French, he was unable to abandon his self-appointed station in Sicily, even though he was urged by Lord Keith to take command of the English force off Minorca, on account of the escape of French and Spanish fleets into the eastern Mediterranean. Over the next two months the liberation of Naples continued to dominate his actions, ending with his collusion in the savage justice meted out by Bourbon loyalists on the Neapolitan jacobins. During July he was recalled to Minorca three times by Keith before finally complying, with his reputation in the British fleet much reduced. In

ABOVE *A ring given by Nelson to Emma; a gold toothpick case which was his Christmas gift in 1804; a gold snuff box inscribed 'Dear Emma from NB' (Nelson and Bronte), and a bloodstone brooch of him which she wore. The 'Nile' ivory toothpick case was his gift to Charlotte Hood and the tortoiseshell box bears a portrait of Emma after one by Madame Vigée-Le Brun*

'A Cognoscenti Contemplating the Beauties of the Antique.' *Sir William Hamilton lampooned as Nelson's cuckold. By James Gillray.*

Nelson eventually considered himself as married to Emma in the eyes of God. Just before he left for Trafalgar they took communion and exchanged betrothal rings in the form of clasped hands. This was his, taken from his body; Emma's is in the Royal Naval Museum, Portsmouth.

August, he was left in acting command of all naval forces in the Mediterranean but he administered this from Palermo and ignored advice to disassociate himself from Emma. On the contrary, early in 1800 they conceived a child.

When Nelson and the Hamiltons arrived in England in November 1800, he was again temporarily reunited with Fanny after a break of nearly three years. But, inevitably, their relationship reached crisis point. Unable to share Fanny's bed, he rejoined the Hamiltons on about 20 November. There was another brief reunion with Fanny after Christmas before he left to join his ship for the Baltic. In March Nelson sent Fanny what she termed his 'letter of dismissal', for by then Emma had been delivered of a baby girl to be named Horatia. He subsequently cut Fanny out of his life, making financial provision for her but returning her letters unopened.

While he was away in the Baltic, Nelson continued to write to Emma, addressing her as Mrs Thompson. She found the house at Merton where he was to spend the brief Peace of Amiens with the Hamiltons. It was, perhaps, the happiest time in Nelson and Emma's relationship. Early in 1802, his niece, Charlotte, stayed with them and Emma proved a loving, careful 'aunt'. Later that year, with Sir William, they toured the mid-west of England and South Wales.

Their *ménage à trois* caused a considerable scandal. They had many tolerant friends but the best society, including the King, would have nothing to do with Emma and only gave Nelson the entrée due to a national hero. Sir William's attitude to his wife's relationship with their companion was remarkable. It was not until about September 1802, after returning from their tour, that his urbane patience cracked. Even then he could still only communicate his views to Emma in a letter and remained loyal to his friend Nelson. Though he protested at the social life and expense to which he was put by living at Merton, he was 'determined not to have more of the very silly altercations that happen too often between us and embitter the present moments exceedingly'. He felt:

that the whole attention of my wife is given to Lord N. and his interest at Merton .... I well know the purity of Lord N.'s friendship for Emma and me, and I know how very uncomfortable it would make his Lordship, our best friend, if a separation should take place, and am therefore determined to do all in my power to prevent such an extremity, which would be essentially detrimental to all parties, but would be more sensibly

The silver collar of Nileus, one of Nelson's dogs.

HORATIA

Nelson and Lady Hamilton's daughter was born at the end of January 1801 and was put out to the care of a Mrs Gibson until after Sir William's death. Nelson and Emma had already devised an elaborate charade that she was in fact the daughter of a seaman called Thompson to whom they were godparents and whom Nelson subsequently 'adopted' as an orphan. Nelson was extremely good with children and both he and Emma adored Horatia. He last saw her on the night he left Merton in September 1805 and one of his last wishes was that she should adopt the name of Nelson. This she did and in 1813 went with Emma to Calais. Here, despite her own problems, her mother scrupulously did her best for the girl, for whom Nelson had left an allowance. On Emma's death, when Horatia was fourteen, she returned to the care of his family who were equally kind to her. In 1822 she married the Reverend Philip Ward, vicar of Tenterden, Kent, who afterwards changed their name to Nelson-Ward. They had nine children and Horatia died aged eighty in 1881.

Horatia never knew who her mother was. Emma always refused to say and though she knew Nelson was her father, Horatia's gravestone still formally proclaimed it an adoptive relationship. It was only in 1887 that the emergence of Nelson's letters to Emma placed the facts beyond debate.

A miniature of Horatia, probably in the early years of her marriage, by James Holmes (1777-1860).

Horatia Nelson, aged ten: marble bust, by Christopher Prosperi (active 1800-15), exhibited at the Royal Academy in 1812.

This necklace was a gift from Nelson to Horatia; she asked him for a dog, and he sent her the gold one in this form. The red box holds her wedding ring.

A photograph of Horatia in 1859, just after she was widowed, showing a strong resemblance to her father.

"Ah,where, & ah where, is my gallant Sailor gone? — He's gone to Fight the Frenchmen, for George upon the Throne} DIDO, in Despair! {He's gone to fight ÿ Frenchmen, I loose t'other Arm &Eye. And left me with the old Antique, to lay me down & Cry.

felt by our dear friend than by us.[23]

Sir William was to die seven months later, in April 1803, with both Emma and Nelson at his bedside.

When they might have at last been alone, war resumed and Nelson was recalled to sea. But absence only seemed to reinforce his love for Emma and his daughter: 'be assured that I am thinking of you and her every moment. My heart is full to bursting.'[24] Early in 1804, Emma was delivered of another daughter, who died before she could be christened. Nelson was to return to Emma at Merton in August 1805, when to Lord Minto the passion seemed 'as hot as ever'.[25] He

'Dido in Despair': Gillray's unflattering caricature of Emma lamenting Nelson's departure for the Baltic in 1801, while on the other side of the bed Sir William Hamilton sleeps on. The classical allusions are to the desertion of Dido, Queen of Carthage, by her lover Aeneas, and to Sir William's passion for antiquities.

had to leave again at the beginning of September. 'I love and adore you to the very excess of the passion,' he wrote from the *Victory* in the Channel. 'Kiss dear Horatia a thousand times for me.'[26] Emma was equally devoted to her daughter and to Nelson: 'Oh Nelson, how I love her but how I do idolize you – the dearest husband of my heart, you are all in this world to your Emma.'[27]

When the French and Spanish fleets were in sight off Cape Trafalgar, one of Nelson's last acts was to make a new will in which he asked, should he die, that Emma and Horatia be provided for by his country: 'these are the only favours I ask of my King and Country at this moment when I am

JOHN BULL taking a Luncheon: — or — British Cooks, cramming Old Grumble-Gizzard, with Bonne-Chére.

going to fight their Battle.'[28] On his death, his brother William received an earldom, £99,000 for an estate and an annual pension of £5,000 a year, while Fanny received an annual pension of £2,000. Emma and Horatia were given nothing.

NELSON AND THE PUBLIC

The vast attendance at Nelson's state funeral is evidence of the regard with which he was held by the public, and in his lifetime he received more adulation than is now generally given to monarchs. The acclaim was international. Coming back from Italy in 1800 he was watched and cheered by crowds everywhere he passed. It was the same in England. In 1802, Charlotte Nelson

'John Bull taking a Luncheon'. The public appetite for victories after the Nile: Nelson leads other naval heroes of his time in serving up 'frigasees' of Britain's enemies to John Bull, while Fox and the Whig political opposition fear for their skins outside.
By James Gillray.

watched her uncle going to the Guildhall during the Lord Mayor's show in London. Amid the noise and confusion, the carriage in which Nelson, the current and the last Lord Mayor were sitting, was relieved of its horses and drawn on by the crowd. There were 'people jumping up to the carriage to see my Uncle and thousands of people round him looking at him... all the ladies had their handkerchiefs out of the windows when my uncle passed, they and the people calling Nelson for ever.'[29]

The adoring public included members of the nobility. After the Battle of the Nile, Lady Spencer, wife of the First Lord of the Admiralty, could hardly contain herself: 'Joy, joy, joy to you,

His sycophancy was ill-judged: the Prince had no naval influence and Nelson gained no help from him, though he did seek it. It is likely that George III, whose relations with his sailor son were poor, disapproved of his friendship with Nelson or its embarrassing naval consequences. This may partly explain why Nelson failed to get a ship between 1787 and 1793. He continued to write to the Prince for the rest of his life, however, and once he realized that he could be of little help, the correspondence became less self-conscious. As his reputation grew, their roles reversed and the Prince became more deferential to Nelson.

Sir George Cockburn, Admiral of the Fleet (1772-1853). Nelson's protégé, captain of La Minerve *when they took the* Santa Sabina *together, and the man who in 1815, in the* Northumberland, *took Napoleon to his last exile on St Helena. From a portrait showing him as a rear-admiral in 1817, by John Iames Halls (d.1834)*

Deference to princes was of course normal in an age when all patronage ultimately sprang from the Crown. Demonstrations of dependence were also usual in an organization that functioned on personal service and recommendation. Nelson himself was treated in a similar manner by the able younger men who came within his influence. Captain George Cockburn was perhaps the most able, serving under Nelson in the Mediterranean from July 1795 to April 1797, when he was sent on a cruise with Captain Benjamin Hallowell. It was, he wrote to Nelson, 'the thing of all others most to my liking...

considering I was too late to be with you', and he was still keen to return to Nelson the following July: 'next to my own father, I know of none whose company I so much wish to be in or who I have such real reasons to respect'.[33]

Although real affection lay behind Cockburn's comments, the more tangible reasons for this respect included a mutual share in prize money, itself the product of successful co-operation. In 1795-6 Nelson often left his squadron under the command of Cockburn in the Gulf of Genoa, while he liaised with the Austrian army on shore and reported to Jervis, the naval commander-in-chief. The task was to disrupt supplies along the coast to the French army creeping into northern Italy and, within a year, Nelson could rest 'perfectly assured' in leaving the work to Cockburn, 'the particular nature of which you so well know.... We so exactly think alike on points of service that if your mind tells you it is right, there can hardly be a doubt but I must approve.'[34] Cockburn's immediate reward was a larger ship:

Captain Sir William Hoste (1780-1828). Hoste was one of the Norfolk boys whom Nelson took to sea and promoted. Just before Trafalgar, he sent him off in command of a frigate and Hoste missed the battle. He was deeply disappointed but in 1811, commanding a frigate squadron, brilliantly defeated superior forces at Lissa in the Adriatic, flying the signal 'Remember Nelson'. From a portrait by Samuel Lane (1780-1859).

the 42-gun *La Minerve*, captured from the French, for which Nelson pestered Jervis on Cockburn's behalf.

Nelson gained much from the assistance of such a subordinate. It was in *La Minerve* in December 1796 that he sailed as commodore to undertake the evacuation of Elba. Five days from Gibraltar *La Minerve* encountered, fought for two hours and took the Spanish *Santa Sabina*, only to have her retaken by a superior Spanish force. The manoeuvres and action gained Nelson credit, for as commodore he directed the event. Nevertheless, Cockburn had trained the crew and managed the ship and it was a partnership Nelson generously acknowledged. He continued to hold up Cockburn as an exemplary officer deserving of every opportunity. In 1799 he again employed him 'for service of head' and put him on a station most remunerative in the way of prizes. Until 1802, in England, they continued to meet to settle prize-money accounts, for which Cockburn was given the responsibility.

Sir Thomas Masterman Hardy, Vice-Admiral of the Blue (1769-1839). He was temporarily Nelson's flag-captain after the Nile, filling the role permanently from 1801 and doubling as Captain of the Fleet in Victory at Trafalgar. He frankly told Nelson that the success of their relationship was 'my always being first lieutenant when you like to be captain, and flag-captain when you have a fancy for being admiral'. 'Kiss me, Hardy', said the dying Nelson; the undemonstrative Hardy did, and a second time in farewell. He was later First Sea Lord and Governor of Greenwich Hospital, where he is buried. This shows him, still a captain, in 1807. By Domenico Pellegrini (1759-1840).

Nelson made friends of many of his subordinates. He took an avuncular interest in the young midshipmen and 'captain's servants' on board his vessels, whom he termed 'his children' and attempted to encourage and educate. In 1793 he took a group of Norfolk boys to sea with him, including his stepson Josiah Nisbet and William Hoste, also the son of a parson. In 1802 the latter acknowledged that Nelson had 'taken me by the hand from my first entrance into the service and has never ceased his good offices till he has got me a post-captain's commission'.[35] Many others also owed their careers to Nelson's patronage, Sir Thomas Hardy among them; he initially served as a lieutenant under Cockburn, before being given a command by Nelson.

Nelson actively cultivated these friendships with professional colleagues. They were, after all,

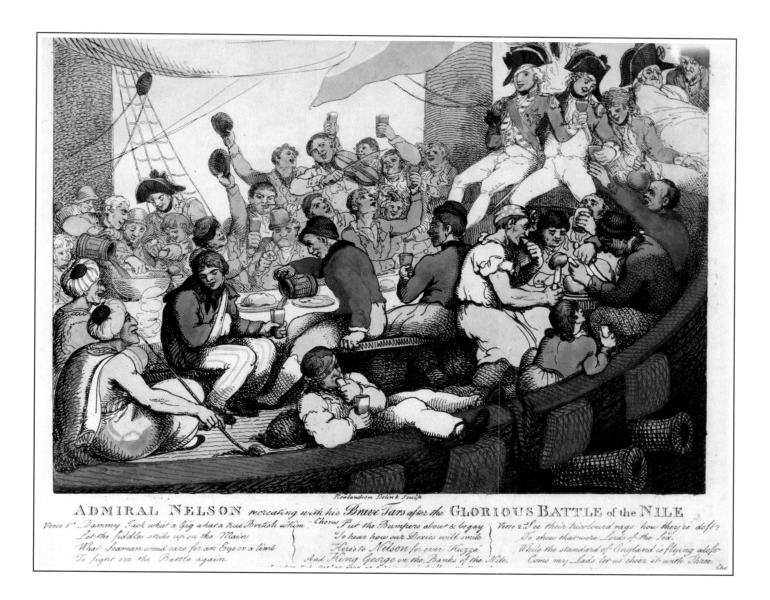

ADMIRAL NELSON *recreating with his* BRAVE TARS *after the* GLORIOUS BATTLE *of the* NILE

Verse 1st Dammy Jack what a Gig what a true British whim
Let the fiddles strike up on the Main
What Seaman would care for an Eye or a limb
To fight o'er the Battle again.

Chorus Put the Bumpers about & be gay
To hear how our Dexies will smile
Here's to *Nelson* for ever Huzza"
And *King George* on the Banks of the Nile.

Verse 2nd See their tricoloured rags how they're doft?
To shew that were Lords of the Sea.
While the standard of England is flying alasor
Come my Lads let us cheer it with Three.
                                                    Cho.

useful to him. The enjoyment and mutual benefits of camaraderie were encouraged by Nelson's habit of socializing for a while each evening. After tea at seven, he would send for 'my family, to sit and talk' until punch, cake or biscuit at eight, over which he generally 'unbent himself'.[36] It was no doubt at gatherings such as these that Nelson ensured that his subordinates perfectly understood his tactical intentions, whatever the

'Admiral Nelson recreating with his Brave Tars after the Glorious Battle of the Nile.' *Rowlandson's print of 1800 with a song attached.*

circumstances in which they should meet an enemy. His 'band of brothers' were originally those who fought with him at the Nile but, effectively, the circle grew wider.

Some of the officers he worked with became special friends, Collingwood being the most important, though ten years older. Their paths first crossed as lieutenants in 1778 and Nelson had been able to relate to the big, rather diffident

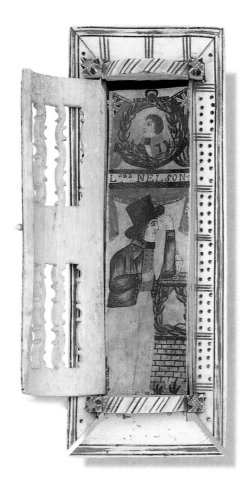

The inside of this bone domino box shows a British sailor mourning at a bust of Nelson, a common theme in commemorative pieces after Trafalgar. This is one of many items made and sold by French prisoners of war in England to earn a small income.

man in the most relaxed of manners. They had a mutual friend in Mary Moutray and corresponded to the end of Nelson's life. Collingwood observed in 1798 how, having served and lived together for 'many, many years... all that ever happened to us strengthened the bond of our amity'.[37] As an admiral, he was second-in-command at Trafalgar, where his flagship *Royal Sovereign* was the first ship in action.

NELSON'S MEN

Nelson also commanded a unique strength of affection amid the ordinary seamen of the fleet, a society of men whose sentimentality could be as remarkable as their tough independence. He had a special relationship with some, such as John Sykes, his coxswain, who twice saved his life in a boat action off Cadiz in 1797. But with most it was an attachment born of their victories under his leadership. At his first fleet success off Cape St Vincent, though Jervis had the main credit, each ship of the British line gave three cheers as it passed Nelson's shattered *Captain*. The common seaman's affection for Nelson is well known, and seems to have been genuine. He suffered the wounds of action along with his men and he certainly enjoyed and encouraged their attachment. Although a firm disciplinarian, Nelson was a

George Keith Elphinstone, Viscount Keith, Admiral of the Red (1746-1823). A Scot, of long command experience, who fought at Toulon in 1793 and in 1795 took the Cape of Good Hope from the Dutch. In 1798 he succeeded the Earl of St Vincent and Nelson as senior officer in the Mediterranean. Here he disapproved of Nelson's obsession with the security of Naples, his delay in obeying orders and his behaviour with Lady Hamilton. Painted as a vice-admiral, about 1797, by William Owen (1769-1825).

notably humane commander and his achievements vindicated the authority he had over his men. He also knew the advantages of leniency. His ploy of 1787 in using Prince William to grant unauthorized reprieve to a condemned man was not the last instance of this. Just after he had Caracciolo ignominiously hanged for undoubted treason, he stopped the hanging of one of his own men, deliberately at the last possible moment. The offender had struck an officer while drunk; a capital crime, but one for which Nelson judged that the anticipation rather than the deed would be suitable punishment and have better general effects.

NELSON'S SUPERIORS

Just as Nelson used his subordinates, so he was used by his superiors, some of whom became friends. He corresponded with William Locker, his captain in the *Lowestoffe*, until the latter's death in 1800. St Vincent at first found Nelson a valuable asset, Collingwood going so far as to consider Nelson a favourite of his. On the whole, however, his relations with superior officers were uneasy, particularly after the Battle of the Nile. Jealousy certainly had some part in their view of him but it is also evident that Nelson thought he had reached the stage when he could do no wrong. In this, wounds and illness, stress, and his involvement with Lady Hamilton and the politics of Naples all affected his judgement.

To unsentimental officers like Lord Keith, who took over from St Vincent in the Mediterranean, Nelson's conduct was not only foolish but dangerous. As early as April 1799, he noted to his sister that 'the Queen [Maria-Carolina], Lady Hamilton, General Acton and Lord Nelson [were] cutting the most absurd figure possible for folly and vanity' at Palermo.[38] In July Keith intended to pursue the combined enemy fleets out of the Mediterranean and was furious when Nelson wrote back declaring that the safety of the kingdom of Naples depended on him remaining there: 'I have no scruple in deciding that it is better to save the Kingdom of Naples and risk Minorca, than to risk the Kingdom of Naples and to save Minorca. Your Lordship will, I hope, approve of my decision.'[39] Keith did not; nor did the departing St Vincent, nor the Board of Admiralty who formally reprimanded Nelson, in sharp contrast to King Ferdinand, who awarded him a Sicilian dukedom for his conduct.

With Keith, Nelson's professional reputation reached rock-bottom. Nelson wanted to take the Hamiltons back to England in the *Foudroyant* but Keith refused to let him remove a useful ship and was undoubtedly influenced by comment throughout the western Mediterranean about his conduct with Emma. The British Consul at Leghorn complained that 'Lady Hamilton has had command of the fleet long enough'.[40] When the distinguished soldier Sir John Moore saw Nelson 'covered with stars, ribbons and medals', he thought him 'more like the Prince of an opera than the Conqueror of the Nile. It is really melancholy to see a brave and good man, who hast deserved well of his country, cutting so pitiful a figure.'[41] Keith echoed these sentiments: 'I am grieved, as every one must be, that a man who on other occasions has done so well should on this have so sadly exposed himself to ridicule and censure.'[42]

Back in England, St Vincent heartily disapproved of the liaison with Emma. In November 1800, after Nelson and the Hamiltons had returned from Italy overland, he wrote to Sir Evan Nepean, the Secretary of the Admiralty:
It is evident from Lord Nelson's letter to you on his landing that he is doubtful of the propriety of his conduct. I have no doubt he is pledged to getting Lady H.

The HERO   of the NILE.

'The Hero of the Nile.'
Gillray catches the vanity of
Nelson's appearance after the
Nile, weighed down by his
sword, with the chelengk
and sable-trimmed pelisse
awarded him by the Sultan.
Nelson's motto ('Let he who
has earned it bear the palm')
appears below his satirized
coat of arms, including loaded
money bags and the legend
'£2000 per annum' — the
government pension which
came with his barony.

NAVAL MEDALS

The practice of awarding official naval campaign medals began in 1794 with the gold medals given to captains and flag-officers at Howe's victory of the Glorious First of June. The same pattern, to a design of Thomas Pingo, was awarded for later fleet actions of the French Wars. Private medals for the Battle of the Nile were also distributed to officers and men by Nelson's banker, Alexander Davison, and for Trafalgar by Matthew Boulton, the industrialist. However, it was only in 1848 that Queen Victoria instituted a Naval General Service Medal which all who had fought in recognized actions could claim retrospectively. This was the first official medal for men and junior officers.

ABOVE AND BELOW RIGHT
The obverse of Alexander Hood, Lord Bridport's, flag-officer's gold medal and chain for the Battle of 1 June 1794 and the reverse of Collingwood's for Trafalgar. The chains awarded in 1794 were not repeated, subsequent medals being on blue and silver ribbons. Only 22 were ever issued. Nelson's were stolen in 1900 and lost; that of Rear-Admiral William Carnegie, Earl of Northesk, third-in-command at Trafalgar, was sold by his family in December 1994 for £95,000.

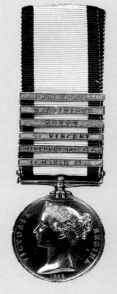

ABOVE *Admiral Sir George Cockburn's Naval General Service Medal with its clasps, including those for his part in Hotham's action in March 1795, La Minerve's capture of the Santa Sabina, and for the Battle of Cape St Vincent, 1797.*

ABOVE AND RIGHT
The obverse of a captain's gold medal and ribbon for the Battle of 1 June 1794 and the reverse of Collingwood's identical one as captain of the Excellent *at the Battle of Cape St Vincent, 1797.*

received at St James's [i.e., at court] and everywhere and that he will get into much brouillerie about it.[43]

St Vincent was also in legal dispute with Nelson over prize-money from the Mediterranean. When Nelson visited him in Devon, having just separated from his wife and left Emma pregnant with his child, he was even more critical:

Nelson was very low when he first came here the day before yesterday, appeared and acted as if he had done me an injury and felt apprehension that I was acquainted with it; poor man! he is devoured with vanity, weakness, and folly, was strung with ribbons, medals, etc., and yet pretended that he wished to avoid the honours and ceremonies he everywhere met with upon the road.[44]

St Vincent thought little of Nelson as a practical

This insignia of the Neapolitan Order of St Ferdinand and of Merit is the only one of Nelson's medals to survive. The rest (shown with it and embroidered decorations off his coats in this old photograph) were stolen from the Painted Hall of Greenwich Hospital in December 1900. They were never recovered.

sea officer. On hearing in 1800 that the First Lord of the Admiralty, Lord Spencer, was thinking of putting Nelson in a two-decked ship, he retorted 'if he does, he must give him a separate command, for he cannot bear confinement to any object; he is a partizan, his ship always in the most dreadful disorder and [he] never can become an officer fit to be placed where I am.'[45] He nevertheless had no doubt of Nelson's capacity for leading a fleet in action and approved of his appointment as second-in-command for the expedition to the Baltic, saying he would 'act the fighting part well'.[46] His only fear was that he would 'tire of being attached to a great fleet and want to be carrying on a predatory war (which is his métier) on a coast that he is entirely ignorant of, never having served in those seas.'[47]

Face of a hero. A plaster cast of Nelson's face was made at Vienna in 1800 and was used there as the basis for a bust. The prime mould is lost but this is from a secondary version, with the eyes opened and hair added by modelling.

'Pray let dear Lady Hamilton have my hair...', said the dying Nelson to Captain Hardy. It was cut off after his death and is still tied at the back in this queue or pigtail.

After Copenhagen, there was no question of Nelson again acting as a second-in-command. The upshot of the 'blind eye' incident had been to make Parker look foolish in trying to recall Nelson once he was committed to action. Some must have felt sorry for Parker, but, as Lord Malmesbury realized, 'no wise man would ever have gone with Nelson or over him, as he was sure to be in the background in every case'.[48]

By the time of Trafalgar, Nelson's reputation was what he had made it. In 1795 he had written: 'My character and good name are in my own keeping. Life with disgrace is dreadful. A glorious death is to be envied....'[49] He did not always have a good name, nor was his character admired by all who knew him; but neither did he disgrace himself as a naval officer and he did die a glorious death. It was an end for which his life was preparation. At the news of Trafalgar, Lord Castlereagh – in whose waiting-room Nelson and Wellington had met only three months earlier – told Lord Keith: 'Nelson has terminated his life in a manner worthy of himself'.[50] George III was to put it even more accurately to the dead hero's brother Wiliam, now first Earl Nelson: 'He died the death he wished'.[51]

Marble bust of Nelson, 1801: Nelson's niece Charlotte thought this 'the only true likeness that has ever been made of my dear uncle'. By John Flaxman (1755-1826).

Nelson's Trafalgar vase by Benjamin Smith, London 1807. The Patriotic Fund at Lloyd's awarded fifteen such vases in silver or silver-gilt after Trafalgar, to captains of ships involved or their heirs; others took different rewards. This silver-gilt one, then valued at £500, went to Nelson's brother William, the first Earl Nelson.

THE IMMORTAL MEMORY

HORATIO Nelson, widely known by 1798 but dead before 1806, experienced the sensation of national fame only briefly. His long-term career as a British hero, however, has lasted for nearly two centuries and shows few real signs of fading. The traditional connection between Britain's self-image and the practice of hero-worship has, of course, loosened in recent times: national consciousness depends ever less comfortably on the cult of personality.[1] But Nelson's role in defining national identity has undoubtedly been significant, and his place in our culture remains strong and pervasive. It has been kept there chiefly by means of monuments, paintings, prints, poems, books, plays, exhibitions, films, names of streets and public houses, merchandise, turns of phrase and other media which continue to propagate his name and image.

From the moment his death was confirmed, Nelson's admirers determined that his memory should live forever. The news broke formally in London on 6 November 1805 when a *Gazette Extraordinary* published Collingwood's dispatch to the Admiralty, telling of a great victory tarnished by the loss of 'a hero whose name will be immortal and his memory ever dear to his Country'. The next day the *Morning Post* picked up the theme:

While we mourn at the fate of Britain's Darling Son we have the consolation to reflect that he has closed his career of glory by a work which will place his name so high in the tablets of Immortality, that succeeding patriots can only gaze with enthusiasm, scarcely hoping to reach the envied elevation, which a Nation's tears, to the latest period of time, will drop like so many bright gems upon the page of history, that records the fall of the Illustrious Hero.

Immortal memory and the religious associations it evoked had been a prerequisite of true heroism since Cromwell had claimed divine approval for native patriots in the seventeenth century.[2] This may help to explain the efforts made in the period immediately following Nelson's death to stake his claim to a kind of sainthood. But while his qualities were lauded in print with ever more extravagant superlatives, they were described in the conventional language of heroic virtue, little changed since England's last great military hero, General Wolfe, had died in Canada on the brink of victory over France in 1759.[3] Many of Nelson's obituarists made some effort to place his heroism more closely in a naval context, wherein British seamen were marked, according to Nelson's biographer J. S. Clarke, by 'a never failing love of their country, by humanity towards their fellow creatures, by moderation in victory, by a noble disdain of the severe hardship of their profession, and an elevated sense of its glories'.[4] Nelson was recalled in precisely such terms, putting the weight of tradition behind the

Nelson the hero: one of the most famous portraits, painted in 1798-9, after the Nile, from an earlier sketch. The artist Lemuel Abbott did not know that Nelson's head wound meant he could only wear his hat tipped back off his forehead and had to guess the chelengk's appearance.

the Death of ADMIRAL·LORD·NELSON – in the moment of Victory!

this Design for the Memorial intended by the City of London to commemorate the Glorious Death of the immortal Nelson, is with every sentiment of Respect, humbly submitted to the Right honble the Lord Mayor & the Court of Aldermen

'The Death of Admiral Lord Nelson...Design for the Memorial…': *Gillray's interpretation has Lady Hamilton as Britannia, George III as Captain Hardy and the Duke of Clarence as a 'British tar'. Published in December 1805, it hints at the rush of proposals for monuments.*

The Apotheosis of
Nelson, *by Scott-Pierre-
Nicholas Legrand
(1758-1829).*

claims for his canonization. As the *Courier* of 6 November intoned:

What a man we have lost! how excellent in the choice! how skilful in the combination of the means! how dear in the disposition of his face! how prompt, yet how judicious in his decisions! how cool in the hour of danger! how intrepid, yet how collected on the day of battle; how moderate and magnanimous in the moment of Victory!

Here the stock English heroic virtue of magnanimity in victory was given preference even over the fact that Nelson had actually died. But in the days, months and years to come it was the death in victory – traditionally the most honourable end and bearing the weighty sanction of classical history – on which his heroic claims were to rest most firmly.[5]

Nelson's death none the less gave Britain's enemies some scope for interpreting the Battle of Trafalgar in a different light; for what was perceived in England as a clear victory was not accepted in France or Spain as a clear defeat. Indeed one French report dated 25 October 1805, a propaganda piece in the *Moniteur*, crowed 'Nelson is no more' and affirmed that 'we wait with impatience the Emperor's order to sail to the

NELSON'S FUNERAL

Apart from those of royalty, Nelson's state funeral was the most impressive which had ever been mounted.

After Trafalgar the body was placed in one of *Victory*'s largest water casks, filled from the ship's supply of brandy. At Gibraltar this was topped up with 'spirit of wine' before the jury-rigged flagship sailed for England. She arrived on 5 December at Portsmouth and a week later, on passage to the Downs (off Deal), Dr Beatty performed an autopsy and extracted the fatal bullet from Nelson's back. In the Downs the body was dressed in uniform and placed in a coffin made from *L'Orient*'s mainmast. This was then sealed in lead and a second wooden shell.

> *'Don't throw me overboard, Hardy.'*
> *'Oh, no, certainly not.'*
> *'Then you know what to do....'*

In the middle of Christmas night 1805, a yacht carrying the body arrived off Greenwich Hospital. There, in the funereally draped Painted Hall and a final, magnificently decorated black outer coffin, the hero lay in state from the 4th to the 7th January 1806 while huge numbers of people filed past to pay their respects. On 8 January the body was carried by seamen from *Victory* to a black-canopied funeral barge. In a two-mile river procession, it was then rowed against a stiff south-west wind up the Thames, to rest in the Admiralty at Whitehall overnight.

On the morning of Wednesday 9 January, with all the panoply of

BELOW *The arrival of Nelson's funeral car at St Paul's. After Augustus Charles Pugin (1762-1832).*

RIGHT *John Hoppner R.A.'s ticket to join Nelson's funeral procession from the Admiralty to St Paul's. Hoppner had painted a number of portraits of Nelson.*

FUNERAL
of the late
VICE ADMIRAL
HORATIO VISCOUNT NELSON.
Admit *John Hoppner Esq R.A.*
into the Procession from the Admiralty
to S.t Pauls Cathedral

N.º 642

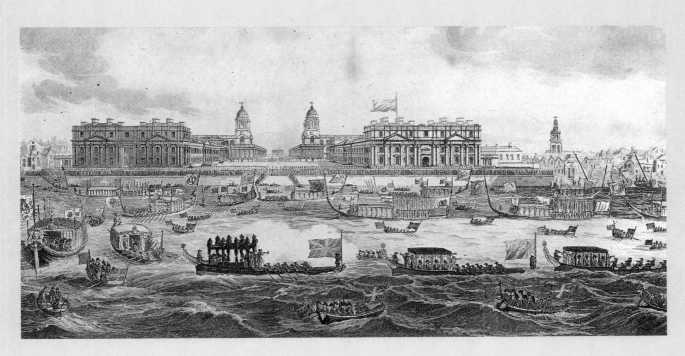

state, the body was borne on an elaborate funeral car to St Paul's Cathedral. The huge cortège included the greatest in the land, with the Prince of Wales and the royal dukes preceding the coffin. People crowded the route from every vantage point and the cavalcade was so long that its tail had not left the Admiralty by the time the head reached St Paul's. There, after a four-hour service, the coffin was lowered to the crypt beneath the centre of the dome. *Victory*'s ensign was buried with it, but not before the seamen of her bearer-party broke discipline and, in an extraordinary scene, tore off and divided a large portion as keepsakes of their admiral.

Nelson's wish to be buried in St Paul's sprang from his being told that Westminster Abbey was built on a marsh, into which it might one day sink. After their deaths in 1810 and 1831 both the other admirals who fought at Trafalgar, Collingwood and Rear-Admiral Lord Northesk, were entombed beside him. In 1813 the Poet Laureate, Robert Southey, wrote:

The death of Nelson was felt in England as something more than a public calamity; men started at the intelligence and turned pale; as if they had heard of the loss of a dear friend. An object of our admiration and affection, of our pride and of our hopes...it seemed as if we had never, till then, known how deeply we loved and reverenced him.

LEFT *Mourning rings and brooch with a lock of Nelson's hair. Fifty-eight such rings, some of which open to reveal a lock of Nelson's hair, were made by John Salter, Nelson's jeweller, for family and close friends attending his funeral.*

LEFT *This miniature lead-lined coffin is inscribed as a gift from Walter Burke, Victory's purser, who supported the dying admiral's pillow. It was made from leftover scraps of lead and wood from the second and third coffins inside which the body was enclosed before leaving Victory.*

NELSON'S FUNERAL

RIGHT *The figurehead of Nelson's funeral carriage, representing Fame with a laurel wreath, and two of the letter A's from the canopy inscription. The carriage remained in the Painted Hall at Greenwich until 1840 but was then dismantled.*

BELOW *Nelson's funeral in St. Paul's. On a dark January afternoon the whole interior of the dome had to be artificially lit for the first time in its history. Among the enemy flags displayed was the Spanish ensign shown on page 60. After A.C. Pugin.*

A selection of the many cheaply produced transfer decorated mugs, jugs and other crockery made to commemorate Trafalgar and Nelson's death.

enemy's shores, annihilate the rest of his navy, and thus complete the work we have so brilliantly begun'. Napoleon had, in fact, postponed his English invasion plans just before Trafalgar and by Christmas may justifiably have felt that the autumn's most important events had been the Austrian surrender at Ulm, on 22 October, and his defeat of the combined Russian-Austrian army at Austerlitz on 2 December. The far-reaching effect of Trafalgar on Britain's national security was not to become completely apparent, either at home or abroad, for some years yet; the victory was initially seen not so much as a turning point in history as an occasion for a kind of triumphal mourning.

Even before the extraordinary funeral ceremony in January 1806, the first of the many commemorative projects which were to enshrine Nelson's name and reputation were already emerging. Early examples before the close of 1805 included several theatrical re-enactments of his life, numerous hastily produced portrait prints, crude medals, an engraved representation of Lady Hamilton as Britannia crowning the head of Nelson and even a full-scale monument in Ireland reputedly erected by 10 November. There were immediate and widespread plans for commemorative monuments. This was partly because Parliament had recently resolved to fund a series of statues of naval and civil heroes, but many of the proposals in autumn 1805 reflected new initiatives.[6] The over-wrought and predictable nature of many entries submitted for one City of London competition was aptly caricatured by James Gillray's print of 23 December in his none the less affectionate account of early

Two engraved rummers: that on the left commemorates Trafalgar and Nelson, the other shows his funeral car.

English responses to Nelson's loss (see page 146). Meanwhile, Nelson's body had arrived home and was brought to Greenwich to lie in state in the Painted Hall, while preparations for a funeral of unprecedented pomp and spectacle were underway – the nation's symbolic affirmation of his significance, complementing the parliamentary grants of title and annuities to his family.

The Painted Hall was opened to the public on 5 January 1806, and up to 100,000 mourners were said to have passed by the body over the next three days. On the 8th, amid booming guns, tolling bells and tearful crowds, the coffin was taken by barge to Whitehall and thence to the Admiralty. On the 9th a procession of 160 carriages set out for St Paul's Cathedral, where Nelson was to be entombed at public expense in an extravagant Renaissance sarcophagus, once intended for Cardinal Wolsey. It was a day of spectacle, internationally reported. There were tales of open and private grief, of the comportment of Nelson's fellow officers, his men, friends,

strangers and even of supernatural intervention in the proceedings. By all accounts it was one of the most remarkable public events London had ever witnessed, redolent with the imagery of sainthood, patriotism, national and naval pride and sanctioned by popular participation.[7] By also establishing a visual dimension to Nelson's claim to historical superstardom, it also opened up a great range of commercial opportunities for artists, sculptors, craftsmen, print-sellers, writers, publishers and entrepreneurs of every kind, in whose hands Nelson's best chance of immortality was to lie. Appropriately, his own ostentatious and career-minded theatricality in manner and deportment was now matched by the ambitions of a burgeoning arts industry.

Naval victory and heroic martyrdom were a powerful combination with great marketing possibilities. A demand for commemorative merchandise had already been sharpened by naval successes of the French wars, putting the names of Admirals Howe, Jervis, Duncan and others

These Doulton stoneware commemorative jugs were produced to celebrate the centenary of Trafalgar in 1905.

into households at practically all social levels, but the industry now reached new heights.[8] Every last detail – or alleged detail – of Nelson's life, the Trafalgar campaign and the funeral rapidly found its way into some form of mass production. Images of Nelson's face, of the *Victory* (or sometimes of quite different people and ships) and of his coffin, were rapidly reproduced in a variety of media and adorned with patriotic slogans for mass consumption. There were cheap transfer-printed pottery mugs and jugs at one end of the market; fine porcelain and engraved glass at the other. There were snuff boxes and patch boxes, stoneware bottles and linen squares, toothpick cases and ladies' fans, enamelware and furniture. The famous signal 'England expects that every man will do his duty', or variants of it, and hastily penned doggerel ('Rule brave Britons, rule the Main/Avenge the Godlike hero slain') were habitually added by way of narrative. And, for those who wanted to look at merchandise rather than buy it, makeshift displays were set up

in many towns and cities, revealing in exchange for an entrance fee the latest engraved prints or other new Nelson products on the market.[9]

The print trade had been developing fast since the 1760s and was stimulating an expanding market for representations of recent British history. It now tackled new Nelsonic opportunities with vigour.[10] Two basic kinds of image began to emerge. First, there were episodes from Nelson's life, tending to present his career as a series of heroic acts. These were to become notably influential much later in the nineteenth century, but the best-known early set was engraved after the paintings by Richard Westall in 1807 and published as book illustrations in J. S. Clarke and John M'Arthur's *Life of Nelson* (1809), the first full biography. The second kind were images of Nelson's death. For these there were several his-

A mid-nineteenth-century Staffordshire chimney group of the death of Nelson.

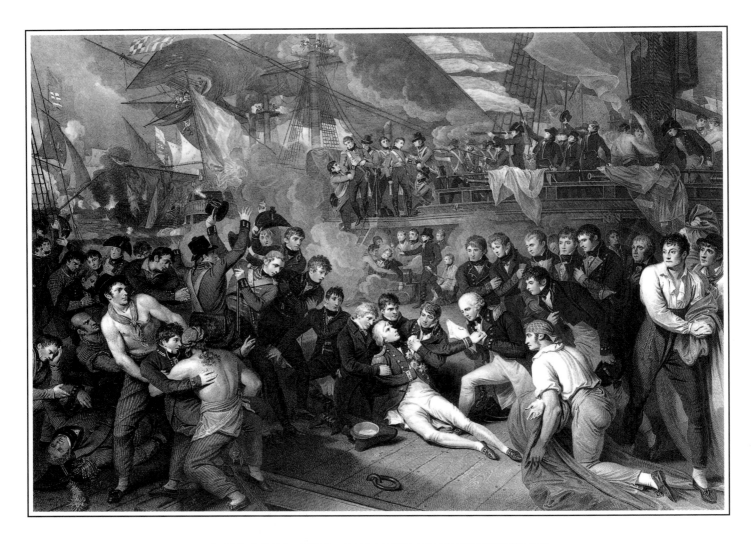

ABOVE
James Heath's hugely
successful print of 1811 after
Sir Benjamin West's painting
of the death of Nelson, now
in Liverpool. Nelson himself
told West that he always
stopped to admire prints of
his Death of General
Wolfe *(left), and hoped West*
would record his own death
if he died in action.

torical and visual precedents on which to draw. There had already emerged a tradition of 'death tableaux', with its own rules and conventions, into which the portrayal of Nelson's last moments was now somewhat unimaginatively inserted. Today the most familiar image of his death is probably that by Arthur William Devis, painted in 1805–7 and published as a print in 1812 by Josiah Boydell (see page 112). Its main ingredients broadly matched the many contemporary written accounts, set below decks with the wounded hero surrounded by his colleagues and attendants. But the best-selling print in the early years after the event was actually that by Benjamin West, which deliberately departed from the known facts of Nelson's death. Painted in 1806–7 and engraved and published by James Heath in 1811, it repeated the basic formula seen in West's own *Death of Wolfe* (1770) and was conceptually related to John Singleton Copley's *Death of Major Peirson* (1784) and several other well-known death scenes of the period.[11] West and Copley in particular were developing a strong feeling for what the public wanted – their pictures earned them several thousand pounds from special exhibitions even before they were

The Immortality of Nelson *by Sir Benjamin West (1738-1820): the hero offered up to Britannia by Neptune. Exhibited at the Royal Academy in 1807 as part of West's concept for a monument.*

reproduced as prints to earn yet more. Central to their intention, as West affirmed, was the elevation of the subject from fact to epic. He was very disparaging of Devis's rival effort, arguing that: *there was no other way of representing the death of a hero but by an Epic representation of it. It must...excite awe and veneration.... Wolfe must not die like a common soldier under a bush; neither should Nelson be represented dying in the gloomy hold of a ship, like a sick man in a prison hole....No boy would be animat-*

Lifesize wax effigy of Nelson by Catherine Andras, commissioned by Westminster Abbey to draw fee-paying visitors. Lady Hamilton made an emotional visit with Horatia to see it and testified to the accuracy of the resemblance.

ed by a representation of Nelson dying like an ordinary man. His feelings must be roused and his mind inflamed by a scene great and extraordinary. A mere matter of fact will never produce this effect.[12]

Clearly no potentially immortal hero could afford to be portrayed 'like an ordinary man' and West's picture cited its religious references conspicuously: Nelson's dying pose, like Wolfe's, was drawn from Renaissance 'lamentation' traditions by way of Van Dyck. Devis's image, though scorned by his rival for its supposed factual accuracy, also presented the hero lying and dying in a manner richly evocative of a descent from the Cross.[13] Next, almost inevitably, came images of Nelson rising again. Most were in the form of concept designs for monuments: for example, *The Apotheosis of Nelson* by Legrand and *The Immortality of Nelson* by West, in which Neptune drapes his dead son over the knees of Britannia. The latter was published in 1809 as the frontispiece to Clarke and M'Arthur's *Life* but was actually executed too, in modified form, as sculpted decoration on the portico of the King William Court of Greenwich Hospital. Whether in heaven or in the Temple of Fame, Nelson seemed safely immortal.

His earthly manifestations also continued to multiply. One of the best known was the life-size wax effigy by Catherine Andras, supposedly so life-like that it moved Lady Hamilton to tears.[14] This was bought and installed in Westminster Abbey in 1806 in order to lure tourist traffic away from Nelson's tomb in St Paul's Cathedral. St Paul's responded in 1807 by commissioning John Flaxman's monument to Nelson, finally installed in 1818, whose narrative revolves on the theme of Britannia showing the hero's example to a young seaman.[15] By the 1820s, some worries about the state of the Navy – now smaller in peace time – may have been responsible for the shift of focus in images and monuments towards the living figure of Nelson and his example to the future, rather than on the manner of his death. There was, however, one great visual essay on the death still to come: J. M. W. Turner's enormous *Battle of Trafalgar* commissioned by George IV for St James's Palace in 1822 and hung in 1824 (see page 110). Here, from the perspective of an era far less confident that peace and victory naturally bred glory and prosperity – for the post-war years had brought economic hardship to many – Turner explored the darker side of heroic death. Nelson, just visible on the *Victory*'s deck, is shown about to fall in the name of Duty, with this last word of his famous signal spelt out in the flags of the collapsing foremast, while blood and dying sailors pollute the sea in the foreground. The picture, not surprisingly, was never popular with the Navy, and after its transfer in 1829 to the new 'National Gallery of Naval Art' at Greenwich Hospital it became a well-known focus of controversy and discussion for the Pensioners there.[16]

The ambiguity of heroic example pondered by Turner was not a widely discussed theme, though the tortuous history of the commissioning and building of Nelson's Column in Trafalgar Square does suggest that Nelson's final enshrinement as a truly national symbol met with less than total commitment. Earlier monuments to him around the country had been financed by enthusiastic local communities, expressing their own civic pride through the celebration of a national hero; but by the late 1830s, public subscriptions for the London monument had been unimpressive. Though the design competition launched by the Nelson Memorial Committee in 1838 attracted 124 entries, 40 models and a great deal of debate over their relative merits, one committee member feared that the project might 'become an instance of miserable national parsimony'. In the end, approximately 1,500 subscriptions were received, ranging from a donation of 500 guineas from Queen Victoria to two shillings and sixpence from one Mrs Beeby, and enough was banked to start construction of the approved scheme. The monument and column were designed by William Railton and the statue by Edward Hodges Baily. There were many contractual and financial disputes to come, and with Sir Edwin Landseer's sculpted lions added as late as 1867, the project took nearly thirty years to complete.[17] Thanks to the column, a way had at last been found to keep Nelson in the heavens and on public show at the same time, even though the wranglings to get him there had hardly added lustre to his name.

Nelson's reputation fluctuated during the course of the century according to the political or social tenor of the moment. For a while, after Wellington's victory at Waterloo in 1815, he became half of a kind of heroic double-act, naval

Monument to Nelson in St Paul's Cathedral by John Flaxman (1755-1826). Sir William Hamilton introduced Nelson to Flaxman as 'the sculptor who ought to make your monument'. 'Is he?', said Nelson, 'then I heartily wish he may.'

ABOVE *Carving E. H. Baily's statue of Nelson for Trafalgar Square, 1842. The 17ft (5.2m) figure in Craigleith stone was placed on the column on 3-4 November 1843; this drawing is by Baily himself (1788-1842).*

LEFT *Nelson's Column today: it measures 162ft 6in (50m) to the top of the statue.*

and military celebrity honoured together in image and prose.[18] Having died at the moment of victory, however, Nelson did have the upper hand over Wellington. The great soldier was not only unfashionably aristocratic for a popular hero, he also lived on as a somewhat less glorious politician for over three decades after his finest hour and died unheroically of epileptic fits in 1852.[19] In the middle of the century, and particularly after the military disasters of 1852-4 in the Crimean War, there was also some shift away from adulation of individual leaders and towards a more sober celebration of the patriotism of ordinary fighting men. This was the seed of focus on the Unknown Soldier, which became well known by World War I.[20] One measure of diminished reverence for Nelson in these middle years was the near-disappearance of Trafalgar Day celebrations, even in the Navy.[21] Against this background, Nelson's own moral shortcomings were more readily acknowledged than in earlier years; his three supposed lapses of character – cruel conduct in Naples, brazen affair with Lady

Hamilton, compulsive vanity – were all debated with a degree of disdain. At this time, with practically no one from 1805 still alive (though the last Trafalgar veteran, Joseph Sutherland, survived until 1890), Nelson's era and even his relevance may have seemed all but lost. In such circumstances, his drop in popularity around the 1850s and 1860s becomes explicable, even if it was by no means complete.

It was also to prove very temporary, for there was to be a remarkable Nelson revival in the last quarter of the nineteenth century. Among the many underlying reasons for this was an apparently renewed conviction in intellectual circles that the history of England was the history of its heroes. National history itself was made a stronger discipline by the publication of a series of landmark surveys by Thomas Macaulay, James Froude, John Green and others in the 1860s and 1870s.[22] A series of great portrait exhibitions in South Kensington from the late 1860s, and the consequent expansion and permanent foundation of the National Portrait Gallery, put the names of England's key historical figures back more clearly into public consciousness. Books about heroes, lists of heroes and debates about who was and was not a hero abounded. The enthusiasm even spread across the Channel: in 1864 Alphonse de Lamartine's adulatory biography of Nelson was published in French. The verdict of G. Barnett Smith in 1899 seemed widely accepted:

In the glory-roll of British heroes no name exercises such a strange fascination as that of Horatio Nelson. The record of his deeds stirs the most sluggish blood and makes the Anglo-Saxon proud of his name and race. He is the boy's hero and the man's hero, from the time when he first steps forth upon the human stage to the sublime moment of his tragic death at Trafalgar.[23]

Nelson's image was once more strong and clear, helped too by the revived use of Nelsonic

ABOVE LEFT *Design for an unbuilt naval monument on Greenwich Hill, by Richard Elsam. The pillar on the left celebrates the Battle of 1 June 1794, that on the right the Nile. Nelson's statue is in the centre, that of Sir James Saumarez, his second-in-command at the Nile, on the right. The spot is now occupied by a statue dating from 1930 of Nelson's hero General Wolfe.*

ABOVE RIGHT *The Nelson Pillar was erected in Sackville Street (now O'Connell Street), Dublin in 1808. In 1966 the IRA blew the statue off the top and the rest was removed. After George Petrie, 1829.*

themes in subject painting and engraving. Richard Westall's interpretations of historical episodes illustrating the 1809 biography were a liberating example to later artists but they appear conservative compared with the output of Victorian painters of historical fiction. G. W. Joy's widely reproduced *Nelson's farewell to his grandmother* of 1883, P. L. Jazet's lurid *Death of Nelson* of 1882 and William Breakspeare's *Nelson and Lady Hamilton in Romney's studio* were some of the examples which played an important role in refamiliarizing the public with the hero's ostensible biography.[24] The part played by Nelson pictures in reinforcing his historical status and in proposing his contemporary relevance is interestingly treated in E. R. Taylor's '*T'was a famous victory*' of 1883, which shows young seamen seeking inspiration from Turner's *Trafalgar* in the National Gallery. The Turner in question is the 1806 picture now at the Tate Gallery, a mild and uncontroversial work by comparison with its 1820s successor. Thomas Davidson's *England's pride and glory* of about 1890 is a variation set in the Naval Gallery at Greenwich Hospital.[25] In both instances the theme of Nelson as an example to admire and emulate was central. Seen much earlier in Flaxman's St Paul's monument, it had featured with varying degrees of emphasis in most of the subsequent Nelson literature. From the 1880s onwards, it began to be accorded a new significance as debates about the condition of the Navy and the quality of its current leadership gathered momentum.

The Navy of 1805 had numbered some 120,000 men; that of 1870, 61,000. By 1888, according to one near-contemporary writer:

the British Navy had sunk to such an alarming condition of weakness, and the want of proper war organization in all departments was so deplorable, that any great naval coalition against us would have cost us the Empire.[26]

Behind such rhetoric lay fierce debates about the scale of funding for the fleet and Nelson was recalled to active service on behalf of the naval lobby. It was time, wrote Rear-Admiral Lord Charles Beresford, that those:

who now hold the power, should realise what Nelson's victories really meant for our country. Nelson was the originator and the embodiment of that idea of 'Sea Power', which has moulded our national life, and kept us in the position of a first-rate Power, wielding a mighty influence in the interests of peace, civilisation, and progress in the councils of the world.[27]

Captain A.T. Mahan's influential biography of Nelson, subtitled *The embodiment of the seapower of Great Britain* (1898), put forward this thesis with particular conviction. During the 1890s Nelson had already made steady gains. He was the star of the 1891 Royal Naval Exhibition at Chelsea (which aimed to demonstrate 'the relation between Britannia's naval expenditure and naval responsibilities') and in 1894 the newly formed Navy League made no secret of its intention to

Nelson and Lady Hamilton in Romney's studio, *by William Breakspeare (1855-1914). Emma's last sittings to Romney were before she left for Naples in 1786, or knew Nelson. This is a product of the late nineteenth-century fashion for often imaginary historical scenes.*

install him as patron saint of its crusade for a bigger, better funded fleet.[28] By 1895 the League had re-established the idea of proper Trafalgar Day celebrations in Trafalgar Square and on 22 October 1896 the *Daily Telegraph* could report a 'national enthusiasm...extraordinary scenes in London' on the previous day. The same reporter noted the 'reluctance of the naval authorities to participate in the occasion' but this was more because of the political implications of the concerted campaign against the Treasury. As the twentieth century approached, Nelson's political career, which in his lifetime had been a short and unimpressive one in the House of Lords, was underway at last.

The potential leverage offered by the approaching centenary of Trafalgar in 1905 was only subtly applied, lest the celebrations appear too warlike for the prevailing fragile peace. The magazine, *The King*, wrote in October 1904:

There was a time, and that not very long ago, when the anniversary might have been the occasion for jubilation,

exultation, and the singing of paeans of triumph and self-glorification. In the entente cordiale of 1905, however, the race hatreds and animosities of 1805…are buried, let us hope for ever.[29]

The *London Opinion* of January 1905 agreed: *The celebration should be conceived in no spirit of blatant Jingoism. The dominant note should be one of profound and fervent thankfulness that England was vouchsafed at the time so puissant a warrior.…The*

ABOVE 'T'was a famous victory' *by Edward R. Taylor (1838-1912). A Greenwich Pensioner engaging two seamen in front of Turner's 1806 view of* Victory *at Trafalgar, then in the National Gallery; painted in 1883.*

occasion should, in fact, be a public holiday throughout the Empire, so that from the humblest to the highest all subjects of His Majesty might be able to sink the antagonisms of the moment in common homage at the shrine of a great hero.

But, continued the same writer, returning to a more familiar theme:

The fact remains that recruiting is not heavy enough, and that our Navy is sadly undermanned. A Nelson

Centenary Celebration would be the means of firing the hearts of lads with a noble ambition, would fan the dying embers of patriotism into a bright flame of enthusiasm, and would be of incalculable benefit to the Navy by emphasising more generous recognition at the hands of the nation.[30]

In the event the celebrations were relatively restrained. There were three exhibitions in London of mainly Nelsonic naval memorabilia (and another organized by a vicar in Dorchester, aimed to 'net a nice sum to help our new organ fund'), a grand ceremony in Trafalgar Square, nationwide church services, tree plantings, special magazine supplements and several new biographies. Of these, S. Baring Gould's was marketed as 'a gift book to Adults, to Schoolboys, to Sailors, and indeed to every class.... A splendid School Prize'. One or two publications aimed to spoil the party: F. P. Badham's *Nelson and Ruffo*, also published in 1905, took issue with Mahan's 'pious reverence for Nelson' and sought to re-open the Naples scandal.[31] However, the newer biographies were notably more liberal in their treatment of Nelson's affair with Lady Hamilton and his reinstatement to the job of universal role model seemed assured. At the Royal Academy, W. L. Wyllie's *Battle of Trafalgar* canvas was exhibited to some acclaim and china manufacturers such as Royal Doulton and Copeland set high standards for the wide range of commemorative material which joined Nelson memorabilia, not all of it authentic, in the marketplace. Unapologetically less distinguished, and pitched cheerfully at a wider market, was the 'Nelson Door Knocker' sold by Gamage's; taking the form of Nelson's figure in miniature, cast in brass, it was to become a best-seller by 1914.[32]

In the years following 1905, however, the centenary commemoration was to acquire a deeper poignancy. As the extent and potential of the German naval build-up became apparent, the fear that England's seapower, her Empire and even her shores, might once more be at risk became widespread. To the pro-Navy lobby this realization was belated but welcome. 'An invasion scare,' wrote Lord Esher to Sir John Fisher, 'is the mill of God which grinds you out a Navy of Dreadnoughts and keeps the British people warlike in spirit.'[33] Even most of the anti-imperialists of the day believed in a strong Navy, and only one, J. M. Robertson, dared to argue specifically that more harm than good came from wallowing in the naval glories of Nelson and an era past.[34] Many others suggested that Nelson and his example had never been more relevant. By 1912, remarkably, an Admiralty-sponsored committee had been set up to investigate exactly how Trafalgar had been won and to see if any of Nelson's tactics could be adapted for modern use.[35] This may seem to speak more of the Navy's imaginative powers in 1912 than of the greatness of its hero but it was not the first or last time that the question 'What would Nelson have done?' was posed. *The Times* published an extensive eulogy of Nelson on Trafalgar Day 1912, stressing the urgency of heeding his example and in 1914, with war breaking out across Europe, the second volume of the *Naval Review* undertook a detailed analysis of 'The source of Nelson's greatness'; it concluded, rather limply, that 'it was due principally to his splendid character'.[36] The issue of British character and the pragmatic advantage of impressing on British sailors the virtues of fearless patriotism, inevitably gathered ground as the war progressed. The Reverend John White's *War Heroes* (1916), a reworking of a 1905 Trafalgar centenary sermon, was among the publications urging the armed forces, to a man, to behave with the selfless courage of Horatio Nelson. His image was called up in the same cause in a 1915

recruitment poster, reminding civilians of the glories of 1805 and asking 'Are you doing your duty today?' (see page 164).

New visual and written interpretations of Nelson's personal and professional life appeared steadily during the Great War years; they ranged from such pictures as Arthur McCormick's *Nelson at the battle of Copenhagen sealing his letter to the Crown* of 1915, portraying a boldly improbable scene of the hero working in a makeshift office on the open deck, through to new biographies and character analyses. A fresh medium, cinema, was now also emerging and Nelson proved a popular subject for early British experiments in film-making.[37] Maurice Elvey's silent *Nelson* of 1918 was a straightforward visual account of his life, inherently and appropriately patriotic for its moment. Bert Haldane's *Romance of Lady Hamilton* (1919) and Richard Oswald's

The Battle of Trafalgar by William Lionel Wyllie (1851-1931). A colour lithograph of 1905, from his oil painting of that year marking the Trafalgar centenary. More than any other, Wyllie's work evokes Britain's imperial naval role at the turn of the century. He was also a major figure in the campaign to preserve the Victory at Portsmouth. The original picture is now in the Royal Naval College, Dartmouth.

Lady Hamilton (1921) crucially shifted the focus on to Nelson as lover rather than commander. Even Walter Summers' *Nelson* of 1926, one of the earliest to attempt some duck-pond battle scenes, paid only passing attention to his naval and national significance. There was some concern that this was a sign of creeping peace-time complacency, though the Navy League kept up its profile and activities and made sure, at least, that Nelson's Column was properly decorated each 21 October. The League also declared Trafalgar Day to be one of remembrance for all sailors lost at sea during the Great War.[38] Nelson's modern image was becoming multi-faceted indeed: tactician extraordinary, symbol of British courage, monument to the dead, Navy patron saint, morally flawed genius, matinée idol. The combination was strong enough to ensure that there was no discernible dip in his popularity during the inter-war years. One sign was the still flourishing Nelson souvenir business; there was even a healthy 1930s industry in faking 1905 commemorative items.[39]

The new twentieth-century Nelson, in all its range, was enshrined during World War II in Alexander Korda's famous propaganda film *That Hamilton Woman* of 1941, starring Laurence Olivier and Vivien Leigh. Conceived with Winston Churchill's input as an effort to counteract pockets of anti-British sentiment in America, it combined stirring romance with a portrayal of a man refusing to give in to dictatorship. The equation of Napoleon with Hitler was not lost on the critics and Churchill expressed satisfaction with the end result, one of

A World War I recruiting poster using Nelson as a variant on the theme 'Your country needs you', 1915.

Hollywood's earliest contributions to the war effort. Recognizing the potency of historical symbols was not of course a British preserve and Nelson was also the focus of some German interest. One rather remarkable feature of Hitler's 1940 invasion plan was revealed in an SS memo of 26 August:

the Nelson Column represents for England a symbol of British Naval might and world domination. It would be an impressive way of underlining the German Victory if the Nelson Column were to be transferred to Berlin.[40]

In an even more involved but intriguing entwinement of Nelsonic imagery with ongoing war, the owner of a version of Lemuel Francis Abbott's famous half-length portrait of Nelson

1805 "ENGLAND EXPECTS" 1915

ARE **YOU** DOING **YOUR** DUTY TO-DAY?

wrote to *The Times* on 26 February 1941 to offer the picture for sale at £1,250 (or £1,000 to the National Maritime Museum) on the following basis:

We feel, at this time, that the picture should be used for benefit of the nation's war effort, and are sure that this would have been in accordance with Lord Nelson's own wishes.... As the Prime Minister has said that the greatest threat to our national existence is the U-boat, it would seem fitting that the purchase money should go towards a special effort against the submarine menace.

Still more recently, in 1966, the enduring political strand in Nelson's compelling emblemat-

ic status was confirmed when the IRA blew up the Nelson Pillar in O'Connell Street, Dublin. In 1808, when it was constructed, one commentator had written that the monument stood as an irritating reminder – to a then indifferent Irish public – of English arrogance, recording only 'the glory of a mistress and the transformation of our senate into a discount office'.[41]

The entanglement of Nelson in politics seems unlikely to diminish as long as he retains some level of association with national prowess. At the same time, the continuing indivisibility of his private life and public image has been central to

Nelson sealing his letter of truce to the Crown Prince of Denmark, by Arthur D. McCormick (1860-1943).

most post-war treatments. In 1948, Admiral Sir William James's *The Durable Monument: Horatio Nelson* declared him 'the only British Admiral whose story is incomplete if his private life is omitted'. James confessed to some irritation in naval circles that this should be the case, but felt it better for the British to warm to Nelson through learning a few salacious personal details than to listen to those – and there still were some – who argued that he was overrated as a commander and as a man. George Bernard Shaw, for example, provocatively suggested that Nelson 'never had to fight a technically capable and properly equipped enemy' and also that he had 'got himself killed by his passion for exposing himself...the result being a tremendous effect on the gallery'.[42] Popular treatments of Nelsonic themes in the 1960s and 1970s frequently focused on his engaging personal mix of strengths and weaknesses. These included the German-made 1968 film, *Lady Hamilton*, a mildly pornographic fiction with an international cast, and the play *The Hero Rises Up* (1968) by John Arden and Margaret D'Arcy, in which Nelson's personal and professional vanities were explored irreverently (some said unpatriotically) in relation to what the public of 1805 seemed to want of him. Terence Rattigan's *Nelson: a study in miniature* (1966), a television play reworked for the cinema in 1973 as *Bequest to the Nation*, starring Peter Finch and Glenda Jackson, also placed Lady Hamilton at the root of Nelson's failure to match his leadership powers with clarity and constancy at home.[43]

Notwithstanding Susan Sontag's recent historical novel *The Volcano Lover*, which re-presented Emma and Horatio for the 1990s, Lady Hamilton seems to have resumed a place to the side, rather than at the centre, of Nelson's memory over the past two decades. This has been expressed partly through a renewed focus on his persona and his navy, not only in the form of good popular books, for example by Tom Pocock, but also in the National Maritime Museum's Nelson galleries (1977–94) at Greenwich, in the Royal Naval Museum and HMS *Victory* at Portsmouth and even in Madame Tussaud's 'Trafalgar Experience' (removed in 1992). Together these have acted for many as modern shrines to a hero and his world. There was also an influential television series in 1982, *I remember Nelson: recollections of a hero's life*; shown just as the Falklands War approached, the last episode focusing on the death at Trafalgar was judged incompatible with the maintenance of good morale in the forces and was postponed until after the war.[44] And lest Nelson's continuing role in today's society still be doubted, each Trafalgar Day 'the Immortal Memory' is toasted at Royal Naval and other dinners across the world, 'keeping the flame alive'. The tradition, intended to argue the enduring relevance of the Nelson example, is for the after-dinner speaker to draw parallels between modern issues and Nelsonic history. In a Trafalgar Day speech in 1989, for example, Prince Charles used Nelson's disregard for naval red tape as a means of drawing attention to the absurdity and potential harm of much government bureaucracy. Casper Weinberger, the former American Defence Secretary, speaking on 21 October 1985, summoned Nelson and his captains in support of his own advocacy of an uncompromising anti-Soviet foreign policy.[45]

Nelson's memory has indeed so far proved immortal, if only through its adaptability to the diverse requirements of a changing world. As the bicentenary of Trafalgar approaches, one thing seems certain: the manner in which he is recalled will depend more on the political and cultural climate of 2005, and on who requires what of him, than on Nelson himself.

England's pride and glory. *By the end
of the nineteenth century the Naval
Gallery in the Painted Hall at Greenwich
Hospital had become a major shrine to
Nelson. The boy is a naval cadet and
all of the paintings shown appear in this
book. By Thomas Davidson
(active 1863-1903).*

NOTES

The main standard works used here are cited as follows (unless otherwise stated all books quoted were published in London):

Elliot
EMMA E.E. ELLIOT-MURRAY-KYNYN-MOUND (ed.), *Life and Letters of Sir Gilbert Elliot, First Earl of Minto, from 1751 to 1808* (3 vols, 1874)

Lavery NN
BRIAN LAVERY, *Nelson's Navy: the Ships, Men and Organisation* (1989)

Naish
G.P.B. NAISH (ed.), *Nelson's Letters to his Wife and Other Documents* (Navy Records Society, 1958)

Nicolas
SIR NICHOLAS HARRIS NICOLAS (ed.), *The Dispatches and Letters of Vice-Admiral Lord Viscount Nelson, 1777-1805* (7 vols, 1844)

Pocock
TOM POCOCK, *Horatio Nelson* (1987)

ABBREVIATIONS:
NMM - *National Maritime Museum* (manuscripts)
NRS - *Navy Records Society, London* (publications)
The names of British and foreign ships in the text are generally rendered in the traditional English spellings; e.g. San Josef not San José.

CHAPTER 1
The Age of Revolutions

1   Strictly, the French Revolutionary War is the period from 1793 to the Peace of Amiens in 1801. The Napoleonic War runs from 1803 to 1815, including the 'Hundred Days' between Napoleon's escape from Elba and his abdication after Waterloo.

CHAPTER 2
Nelson's Navy

1   Marmaduke Stalkartt, *Naval Architecture, or the Rudiments ...of Shipbuilding* (1781; repr. Rotherfield, 1991), **135-6**.
2   A.J. Holland, *Ships of British Oak* (Newton Abbot, 1971), **135**.
3   Brian Lavery, *The Ship of the Line* (2 vols, 1983-84), I, **126**.
4   Edward Pelham Brenton, *The Naval History of Great Britain* (2 vols, 1837), I, **33**.
5   Lavery, *The Ship of the Line*, I, **121**.
6   Quoted in Lavery *NN*, **93**.
7   H.G. Thursfield (ed.), *Five Naval Journals* (NRS, 1951), **8**.
8   *Ibid.*, **11**.
9   Quoted in Lavery *NN*, **93**.
10 *Ibid.*, **119**.
11 C.S. Forester (ed.), *The Adventures of John Wetherell* (1954), **31**.
12 Peter Bloomfield (ed.), *Kent and the Napoleonic Wars* (Gloucester, 1987), 121.
13 Lavery *NN*, **120**.
14 John Bechervaise, *Thirty-six Years of a Sea-faring Life* (Portsea, 1839), **47**.
15 John Nicol, *Life and Adventures* (1822;

repr. 1937), **179**.
16 Christopher Lloyd (ed.), *The Health of Seamen* (NRS, 1965), **265-6**.
17 NMM GRE/15.
18 To his wife, 15 June 1797, in Nicolas, II, **397**.
19 NMM GRE/15.
20 'Memorandum', 9 Oct 1805, in Nicolas, VII, **91**.
21 Thursfield, *Five Naval Journals*, **10**.
22 NMM RUSI/ER/3/**11**.
23 Lavery *NN*, **215**.
24 To Lord Spencer, 6 Sept 1799, in Nicolas, IV, **6**.
25 To Capt. Thomas Troubridge, 7 Sept 1799, *ibid.*

CHAPTER 3
'The Merest Boy'

1   Nicolas, I, 70, n.7.
2   *Ibid.*
3   L.J. Jennings (ed.), *The Croker Papers...1809 to 1830* (3 vols, 1884), II, **233**.
4   Quoted in Pocock, **332**.
5   Quoted in Pocock, **7**.
6   From Nelson's *'Sketch of my life'*, in Nicolas, I, **2**.
7   *Ibid.*
8   See Pocock, 20-21. Nelson's account of his unusual but not unique spiritual experience was noted down from a conversation during his tour in the west and Wales in 1802.
9   Quoted in Pocock, **34**.
10 To William Locker, 23 Jan 1781, in Nicolas, I, **35**.

11 To William Locker, 25 Feb 1783, in Nicolas, I, **71**.

12 To the Revd William Nelson, 29 Mar 1784, in Nicolas, I, **101**.

13 'Sketch...', in Nicolas, I, **9**.

14 To William Locker, 15 Jan 1785, in Nicolas, I, **113**.

15 See Nicolas, I, **294**, n.1.

16 'Sketch...', in Nicolas, I, **11**.

17 To his wife, 7-11 Sept 1793, in Naish, **89**.

18 To Sir William Hamilton, 27 Mar 1794, in Nicolas, I, **378**.

19 To William Suckling, 7 Feb 1795, in Nicolas, II, **4**.

20 To his wife, 18 Aug 1794, in Naish, **119**.

21 To William Suckling, 7 Feb 1795, in Nicolas, II, **4**.

22 To William Locker, 10 Oct 1794, in Nicolas, II, **491**.

23 To his wife, 31 Oct 1794, in Nicolas, II, **493**.

CHAPTER 4
The Decade of Victories

1 To his wife, 1 Apr 1795, in Nicolas, II, **26**.

2 Nelson's draft account of the Battle of St Vincent, in Nicolas, II, **346**.

3 Julian S. Corbett (ed.), *The Spencer Papers* (NRS, 1914), II, **439**.

4 Christopher Lloyd (ed.), *The Nile Campaign* (Newton Abbot, 1973), **20**.

5 Captain Edward Berry to the Revd Dr Foster, 29 May 1798, in Nicolas, III, **18**, n.

6 To his wife, 24 May 1798, in Nicolas, III, **17**.

7 To the Duke of Clarence (Prince William Henry), 10 May 1799, in John Knox Laughton, *Letters and Despatches of Horatio,*

Viscount Nelson (1886), **190**.

8 To Lord Spencer, 6 Apr 1799, in Nicolas, III, **316**.

9 From Colonel Sir William Stewart's account of Copenhagen, reprinted in Nicolas, IV, **309**. Stewart, the prime witness to the incident, commanded the troops embarked as marines.

10 To Sir Evan Nepean, 10 Aug 1801, in Nicolas, IV, **450-1**.

11 John Leyland (ed.), *The Blockade of Brest* (NRS, 1898) I, **344**.

12 Brian Tunstall (Nicholas Tracy, ed.), *Naval Warfare in the Age of Sail* (1990), **249**.

13 Julian S. Corbett (ed.), *Fighting Instructions 1530-1816* (NRS, 1905), **313**; cf. Nicolas, VI, **443**.

CHAPTER 5
'No Common Being'

1 Quoted in Pocock, **273**.

2 Sir George Cockburn to J.W. Croker, 11 Apr 1845, NMM CKE/6.

3 Elliot, III, **370**.

4 *Ibid.*, III, **218**.

5 Oliver Warner (ed.), *Nelson's Last Diary* (1960), **28**.

6 Elliot, III, **374**.

7 To Sir William and Lady Hamilton, 22 July 1798, in Nicolas, III, **47**.

8 To his wife, 10 Mar 1795, in Nicolas, III, **18**.

9 To Revd Edmund Nelson, 19 Oct 1782, in Nicolas, I, **67**.

10 Revd Edmund Nelson to Nelson, 12 July 1793, in Nicolas, I, **319**, n.6.

11 To William Suckling, 14 Jan 1784, in Nicolas, I, **93**.

12 To William Locker, 24 Sept 1784, in Nicolas, I, **110**.

13 To Revd William Nelson, 20 Feb 1785, in Nicolas, I, **23**.

14 To Revd William Nelson, 16 Mar 1785, in Nicolas, I, **126**.

15 To Revd William Nelson, 20 Feb 1785, in Nicolas, I, **123**.

16 A friend to Mrs Frances Nisbet (later Mrs Nelson), c. Jan 1785, in Naish, **12**; see also Nicolas, I, **133**, n.4.

17 To Mrs Frances Nisbet, 19 Aug 1785, in Naish, **16**.

18 To William Suckling, 14 Nov 1785, in Nicolas, I, **144**.

19 See Pocock, **124-5**. Nelson's undated note in French to Adelaide Correglia is in the Huntington Library, California, HM 34180.

20 To his wife, 14 Sept 1793, in Nicolas, I, **236**.

21 To his wife, 16 Sept 1798, in Naish, **399**.

22 To St Vincent, 4 Oct 1798, in Nicolas, III, **144**.

23 Sir William Hamilton to Lady Hamilton, n.d. (c. Sept 1802), in *The Collection of Autograph Letters and Historical Documents formed by Alfred Morrison; the Hamilton and Nelson papers* (2 vols, 1894), II, **197**.

24 Quoted in Pocock, **292**.

25 Elliot, III, **363**.

26 Quoted in Pocock, **317**.

27 *Ibid.*, **321**.

28 Warner, *Nelson's Last Diary*, **29**.

29 Charlotte Nelson to her mother, n.d., in the Bonsor papers, quoted by permission of Sir Nicolas Bonsor, Bt., MP.

30 Quoted in Pocock, **181**.

31 All quotes from the 'Sketch...', in Nicolas, I, **2-5**.

32 To Prince William Henry, 27 July 1787, in Nicolas, I, **250**.

33 Captain George Cockburn to Nelson, 19 Apr, 24 July 1797; British Library Add. Mss. 34,906, ff.28, 205.

34 To Cockburn, 15 May and 20 Oct 1796; Library of Congress, Cockburn Papers, container 13.

35 Quoted in M.J. Rye, 'Nelson's Favourite Protégé: Captain Sir William Hoste....(1780-1828)', in the *Nelson Dispatch*, Jnl. of the Nelson Society, (1983), I, **99-101**.

36 Dr Gillespie, Physician to the Fleet, quoted in J. Winton, 'The Hypochondriac Hero', in the *Trafalgar Chronicle* (1991), I, **28-31**.

37 Edward Hughes (ed.), *The Private Correspondence of Admiral Lord Collingwood* (NRS, 1957), **80**.

38 Christopher Lloyd (ed.), *The Keith Papers* (NRS, 1950), II, **37**.

39 To Lord Keith, 19 July 1799, in Nicolas, III, **414**.

40 Lloyd, *Keith Papers*, II, **62**.

41 *Ibid*.

42 *Ibid*., **214**.

43 St Vincent to Sir Evan Nepean, 9 Nov 1800, NMM AGC/J/6/1.

44 *Ibid*., 17 Jan 1801, NMM AGC/J/6/2.

45 *Ibid*., 9 Nov 1800, NMM AGC/J/6/1. St Vincent was using the point that a two-decker was unusual as a flagship to underline Nelson's restiveness as a subordinate.

46 H.W. Richmond (ed.), *Private Papers of George, Second Earl Spencer, 1794-1801* (NRS, 1924), IV, **264**.

47 *Ibid*., **21**.

48 Elliot, III, **218**.

49 To his wife, 10 Mar 1795, in Nicolas, II, **18**.

50 Lloyd, *Keith Papers* (NRS, 1955), III, **120**.

51 Quoted in Warner, *Nelson's Last Diary*, **20**.

CHAPTER 6
The Immortal Memory

1 See Thomas Carlyle, *On Heroes, Hero-worship and the Heroic in History*, (1840) and J.W.M. Hichberger, *Images of the Army: the Military in British Art*, 1815-1914, (Manchester, 1988), **5**.

2 Carter E. Foster, 'History and heroes: the military narrative in the wake of Benjamin West', pp.47-49, in *The Martial Face: the Military Portrait in Britain*, 1760-1900, David Winton Bell Gallery exh. cat., Brown University, (Providence R.I., 1991).

3 For Wolfe's heroic status and its representation see David H. Solkin, *Painting for Money: the Visual Arts and the Public Sphere* (1993), **207-13**.

4 James Stanier Clarke, *Naval sermons preached on board His Majesty's ship the Impetueux* (1798), **18**.

5 E. Orme and F. Blagdon, *Graphic history of ... Horatio Nelson* (1806), **5**, discusses Nelson in relation to Hannibal and Epaminondas.

6 See Alison Yarrington, *The Commemoration of the Hero, 1800-64: Monuments to the British Victors of the Napoleonic Wars* (1988), **326-43**.

7 Contemporary accounts of the funeral include the official programme in the *London Gazette*, Jan 1806, and *Bell's Weekly Messenger*, 13 Jan 1806.

8 Naval and Nelsonic commemoratives are treated comprehensively in Rina Prentice, *A Celebration of the Sea: the Decorative Art Collections of the National Maritime Museum*, (1994).

9 Broadsheet advertisements were produced on 10 March 1807 for a Norwich showing 'for one week only' of a 'NELSONIAN exhibition, from the Theatre Royal, Covent Garden', organized by one Mr Stretton, and for a similar enterprise in Backhouse's auction room in Hull.

10 Jay A. Clarke, 'Collectors and Consumerism: the British Print Market 1750-1860', in *The Martial Face*, **37-46**.

11 Peter Cannon-Brookes (ed.), *The Painted Word: British history painting, 1750-1830*, Heim Gallery exh. cat. (London 1991), especially **15-70**.

12 Reported by Joseph Farington and quoted in Charles Mitchell, 'Benjamin West's Death of Nelson' in Douglas Fraser *et al.* (eds.) *Essays in the History of Art presented to Rudolph Wittkower* (1967), **270**.

13 *Ibid*., **269**. See also Peter Harrington, *British Artists and War: the Face of Battle in Paintings and Prints, 1700-1914* (1993), especially **85-114**.

14 Geoffrey Callender, 'The effigy of Nelson in Westminster Abbey', in the *Mariner's Mirror* (1941), XXVII, no. 4, **307-13**.

15 See Yarrington, *Commemoration of the Hero*, **41**.

16 The best published summary of the picture is in Martin Butlin and Evelyn Joll, *The Paintings of J.M.W. Turner* (2 vols, 1977), I, **139-40**.

17 See Rodney Mace, *Trafalgar Square: Emblem of Empire* (1976).

18 See Amanda M. Eggars, 'Popularity and Power: Images of the Duke of Wellington', in *The Martial Face*, **53-59**; for Nelson and Wellington see George Russell French, *The Royal Descent of Nelson and Wellington from*

Edward I, (1853), and the British Library 42-volume pamphlet collection *A voice from the tomb. A dialogue between Nelson and Wellington, overheard at St Paul's*, (1853-59).

19 G. Barnett Smith, *Heroes of the Nineteenth Century* (3 vols, 1899-1901), II, **108**.

20 B. Dawn Dunley, 'The Democratization of Military Portraiture in nineteenth-century England', in *The Martial Face*, **75**.

21 Unidentified newspaper cutting from 1879, in A.M.Broadley's *Nelsoniana* collection (British Library; 8 vols, 1902) VII, unpaginated.

22 See Marcia Pointon, *Hanging the Head: Portraiture and Social Formation* (1993), **232-5**.

23 Smith, *Heroes*, I, **5**.

24 Jazet's picture, formerly in the Walker Art Center, Minneapolis, was sold at Sotheby's, New York, 13 Oct 1993; Breakspeare's was sold at Sotheby's, London, 7 October 1980 (lot 142).

25 See *Concise Catalogue of Oil Paintings in the National Maritime Museum* (Woodbridge, 1988), **15**.

26 Charles Beresford and H. W. Wilson, *Nelson and his Times*, n.d. [c.1900], vi.

27 *Ibid.*, iii.

28 For a contemporary insight on the foundation of the Navy League see the *Daily Telegraph*, 22 Oct 1896.

29 *The King*, 22 Oct 1904, **121**.

30 *London Opinion*, 7 Jan 1905, **15**.

31 *Nelson and Ruffo* was written on the premise that 'for the last fifty or sixty years Nelson's English biographers have carefully slurred over the evidence as to an extraordinary warp in their hero's character' (**52**).

32 *Gamage's Christmas Catalogue 1913*, **423**. Gamage's was a then well-known department store and mail order company.

33 Quoted in J.H. Grainger, *Patriotisms: Britain 1900-1939* (1986), **275**.

34 *Ibid.*, 148.

35 For a report on the committee, see *The Times*, 21 Oct 1912.

36 *Naval Review* (1914), II, no.1, **440**.

37 For cinematic portrayals of Nelson see John Sugden, 'Lord Nelson and the Film Industry', in the *Nelson Dispatch* (1986), II, no.5, **83-88**.

38 For uses of Trafalgar Day see for example David Shannon, 'The Nelson Day celebrations of 1928', in the *Nelson Dispatch* (1989), III, no.8, **148-51**.

39 Prentice, *Celebration of the Sea*, **90**.

40 Quoted in Mace, *Trafalgar Square*, 17.

41 Quoted in Mace, *ibid.*, 52.

42 Quoted in James, *The Durable Monument* (1948), **13**.

43 Sugden, 'Lord Nelson and the Film Industry', **86**.

44 *Ibid.*, **86-88**.

45 Weinberger's speech was published in the *Spectator* and reprinted in the *Nelson Dispatch* (1987), II, no.12, **225-8**.

FURTHER READING

Books on Nelson regularly appear but, inevitably, most repackage the familiar story for current tastes rather than adding anything really significant. Two of the most important sources on which all writers draw are Nelson's correspondence, as published by Sir Nicholas Harris Nicolas (see page 168), and the earliest full *Life* (2 vols, 1809) by the Reverend James Stanier Clarke and John M'Arthur. The latter is now largely unreadable but includes unique information from those who knew Nelson, some of which, as in most other books, is requoted here without specific note. Of other pre-1900 works, Sir John Knox Laughton's *Letters and Despatches of Horatio, Viscount Nelson* (1886) is of value both as an abridgement and supplement to Nicolas and as the nearest thing to Nelson's autobiography. It was ingeniously compiled by editing his own writings, as then known, into a continuous narrative, with closely related material and expert comment added where necessary.

The virtue of more recent works given below is that they have been of generally reliable, long-term use to National Maritime Museum staff for reference and as recommendations to readers. The Museum's Library can provide both a longer and more specialized selection.

Among modern popular biographies, Tom Pocock's *Horatio Nelson* (1987) is the first to represent a broad advance on Carola Oman's *Nelson* (1947). However, Christopher Hibbert's *Nelson, A Personal History* (1994), may well become the standard modern 'life', despite deliberate limits on naval detail, through its combination of written merit and full reference apparatus. It appeared after the main text of this book was complete but has proved of considerable background value. The bare specialist details of all Nelson's main sea actions remain those of volumes four and five of Sir William Laird Clowes's *The Royal Navy: a History...* (7 vols, 1897-1903). More general accounts of specific battles include Christopher Lloyd's *St Vincent and Camperdown* (1963) and Oliver Warner's companion volumes on the Nile (1960) and Trafalgar (1959). All were published in a series by Batsford, who also issued Geoffrey Bennett's *Trafalgar* (1977). David Howarth's *Trafalgar: the Nelson Touch* (1969) is another notably well-written account. Dudley Pope's *The Great Gamble: Nelson at Copenhagen* (1972) is a full and circumstantial study of that episode, and Tom Pocock's *Young Nelson in the Americas* (1980) covers an often skimped period in detail.

Shifting the personal focus, Ludovic Kennedy's *Nelson's Band of Brothers* (1951) is a general introduction to Nelson's captains and professional circle, while Lady Hamilton has been the subject of two good modern biographies: *Emma, Lady Hamilton: a Study* by Molly Hardwick (1969) and *Beloved Emma: the life of Emma, Lady Hamilton* by Flora Fraser (1986). *Sir William Hamilton, Envoy Extraordinary* by Brian Fothergill (1969) covers the least celebrated but in some ways most creditably behaved member of the immortal trio.

PICTURE ACKNOWLEDGEMENTS

The Trustees of the Royal Naval Museum, Portsmouth, *27, 28* (top l. and r., bottom r.)
The Science Museum, Science and Society Picture Library, London, *20*
The Scottish National Portrait Gallery, Edinburgh, *9*
The Society for Nautical Research, *81*
Sotheby's, London, *160, 165*
The Dean and Chapter of Westminster, *156*
Greenwich Hospital Collection, NMM, *various*
Drawings: *40-1* by David Hancock, courtesy R.N. Museum, Portsmouth; *80, 85* by Tom Thompson.

The following are NMM photographic references. Pictures may be ordered from the Photo Sales Section, National Maritime Museum, Greenwich, London SE10 9NF (tel 0181-858 4422). The Museum cannot supply images marked ★ without special permission.

Cover: BHC2901. *Frontispiece:* BHC2905. *Page 3:* D6122. *Page 6:* BHC2887.

CHAPTER 1

Page 12 A3255; *13* (top) C1436, (bottom) BHC2711; *14* (top l.) D7661, (top r.) D7662, (bottom) D7317-A; *15* D6813B; *16* (top) A7458, (bottom) BHC2790; *17* (left) C776, (right) A3700; *18* D4695; *21* BHC1097; *22* C9303; *23* (top) BHC1932, (bottom) BHC4227; *24* (top) 9790, (bottom) D5481; *25* (top l.) D5366, (top r.) 2032, (bottom) BHC2529.

CHAPTER 2

26 BHC1096; *28* (bottom l.) D5909; *29* C1109; *30* BHC3675; *31* (top) D7561, (bottom) BHC2637; *32* (top) PW4969, (bottom r.) PW4971, (l.) A5010; *33* (top) PW4968, (bottom) PW4976; *34* BHC1782; *35* A5596; *36* BHC2745; *38* (top) D7562B,

(bottom) BHC2538; *39* (top) D7374, (bottom) BHC1118; *42* (top) D7689-B, (bottom) D7689-C; *43* (l.) D7557A, (r.) D7555; *44* 7301; *45* (top) PAG8550, (centre) A765, (bottom r.) D7689-D; *46* BHC1090; *47* BHC0519; *48* BHC3001; *49* 3646; *50* (top) PAF3812, (bottom) A3320; *51* BHC1005; *52* BHC0470; *53* (top) C260-20, (bottom) PU7765; *54* D7570; *55* (top) D7568, (centre) D7566, (bottom l.) KTP1266, (bottom r.) D7684; *56* (top) D3996-A, (bottom) D4924; *57* D4001-1; *58* D7216; *59* BHC0510; *60* (top) A3391, (below) RP34-3A.

CHAPTER 3

62 BHC2901; *63* (top) C1127, (bottom) D3755B; *64* BHC1772; *65* BHC3045; *66* D7386; *67* BHC2907; *68* PU5965; *69* BHC2846; *70* BHC0421; *71* 5826; *72* BHC2774; *74* A3297; *76* (top r.) A94, (left) D7648-A; *77* BHC3696; *78* (top) 2871, (below) C1175 ★; *81* (left) PAD5480, (right) D7319.

CHAPTER 4

82 D6122; *83* PW5872; *85* (bottom) C1591; *86* (top) BHC0488, (bottom) D7572; *87* BHC0492; *88* (top) BHC0498, (bottom) 2289; *90* (top l.) PU3399, (top r.) BHC2554, (bottom) BHC2528; *91* D7674; *92* BHC0513; *93* (top) BHC0509, (bottom) D4721; *94* (top) D7685, (centre) D4424, (bottom) D7378; *95* (top) D3541, (bottom) 3969; *96* (top l. to r.) D6097, D5921, D6096, (centre) D6105, D6103, (bottom l.) D6109, (bottom r.) D6099, D6093; *97* (all D4861-) (top r.) 11A, (bottom l. to r.) 15A, 5D, 6A; *98* (left) B3173-B, (right) 4933; *99* (top) BHC2895, (bottom) 2374; *100* (top) D7633, (bottom) BHC2756; *101* (top)

BHC0529, (bottom) D7673; *102* (top) D852-2, (bottom) D5828; *103* D7649-B; *104* PW3976; *105* A5505; *106* D7607, (inset) A560; *107* (top) BHC2557, (bottom) D7563; *108* (top) BHC2625, (bottom) BHC0548; *109* PU5717; *110* (top) BHC0565, (bottom) BHC0552; *111* (right) B9701-B; *112* BHC2894; *113* BHC0549.

CHAPTER 5

114 2643; *115* BHC2879; *116* BHC2881; *118* D7318A★; *119* BHC2883; *123* (bottom r.) D7391, (top r.) A4288, (left) D5717; *124* (top) 8252-A, (bottom) D7379; *125* (top) D7375-B, (bottom) PW3876; *126* (top) D5575, (bottom) C3399-A; *127* (top l.) D7573, (top r. and bottom l.) D7377, (bottom r.) D7384; *128* PW3874; *129* C1460; *130* (top) PW3864, (bottom) D7385; *131* (top) D7388, (bottom) D7383; *132* BHC2619; *133* BHC2784; *134* BHC2352; *135* PW3892; *136* D7381; *137* BHC2815; *139* PW3888; *140* (top l.) D5057-2, (bottom l.) D5056-1, (centre) D5067-2, (bottom r.) D5066-1, (top r.) D4675; *141* (right) D7569, (left) C1182); *142* (top) D6591-E, (bottom) D3210; *143* (left) D7636, (right) 2549.

CHAPTER 6

145 BHC2889; *146* B5151; *147* BHC2906; *148* (top) D7393-B, (bottom) 1842; *149* (top) PAH7324, (centre) D7389, (bottom) D7376; *150* (top r.) D5510, (left) D7667, (bottom) B2019; *151* D5854; *152* D6084; *153* (top) D852-5, (bottom) D6073; *154* (top) 3558, (bottom) PAG7700; *155* 2081; *159* (left) PAD3896, (right) PU3914; *160* B41659; *163* D3766; *167* BHC1811.

INDEX

Index compiled by Elizabeth Wiggans